WELCOME to Boulevard Books –
new authors,
new translations,
new experiences.

'Dragons…' by Caio Abreu.
Stories of love and sex, love and
death, love and loss set in the
turbulent cities of Southern Brazil,
told in the graphic but compassionate
style that has made Caio Abreu one
of Brazil's most important younger
writers.

This is the first book in the
'Boulevard Latin Americans' series,
for the best new writing from Latin
America and is the first
English-language edition of Caio
Abreu's work.

Dragons...

Caio Fernando Abreu
Translated by David Treece

BOULEVARD

Dragons...

First published as 'Os Dragoes Nao Conhecem O Paraiso'.
Copyright © Caio Fernando Abreu 1988, by arrangement with
Dr. Ray-Gude Mertin, Literarische Agentur.

Translation copyright © 1990 Boulevard Books. First published 1990 by
Boulevard Books, 14 Lomley House, Tulse Hill, London SW2 2EW,
UK. Tel. ++-44-81-674-2277

The publishers wish to thank Jean-Luc Barbanneau and Edouardo San
Martin for their help in establishing the Boulevard Latin Americans
series. Boulevard Latin Americans and Boulevard Italians are edited by
Ray Keenoy.

ISBN 0 946889 22 8

Boulevard Books are published in the UK in association with Olive
Press/Impact Books and distributed by Harrap Publishing Group.

Cover art by Phil Baines & Tenné Vair.
Typeset by Saxon, Derby.
Printed and bound by the Guernsey Press, Guernsey, C.I.

Dragons...

Contents

I Beauty	1
II The Leaves of Fate Have Fallen	12
III On the Shore of the Open Sea	25
IV Blues Without Ana	30
V Missing Audrey Hepburn	37
VI The Saddest Boy in the World	45
VII The Little Red Shoes	57
VIII A White Sandy Beach, Down by the Gully	70
IX Queen of the Night	80
X Honey and Sunflowers	89
XI The Other Voice	106
XII Little Monster	116
XIII Dragons…	139

I

Beauty

'You've never heard of damnation
you've never seen a miracle
you've never wept alone in a dirty bathroom
and you never wanted to see the face of God.'
(Cazuza: *Only Mothers Are Happy*)

He had to press the bell repeatedly before he could make out the sound of feet descending the stairs. And again he pictured to himself the worn carpet that was once purple, but then had faded to a sort of red and after that turned pink – what colour was it now? – and he heard the tuneless barking of a dog, a nocturnal cough and brisk footsteps. Then he sensed the light switched on inside the house filter through the glass to fall on his face with its three-day-old beard. He put his hands in his pockets, his fingers searching for a cigarette or a key ring to play with while he waited for the little window at the top of the door to open.

Framed by its rectangle, she screwed up her eyes to see him properly. They measured each other up like this – one inside, the other outside the house – until she withdrew, unsurprised. When he entered he saw that she looked older. And more embittered, he later realised.

'You didn't warn me you were coming', she grumbled in that sour old way of hers, which he'd never understood before. But which now, all these years later, he'd learned to translate as 'how-I've-missed-you, welcome, how-nice-to-see-you' or something along those lines. Affectionate, if awkward.

He embraced her stiffly. He wasn't used to touching or caressing. He sank giddily, quickly, into that familiar smell – cigarettes, onions, dog, soap, beauty cream and old flesh that had been alone for years. Taking hold of him by his ears as usual, she kissed him on the forehead. Then she reached out her hand and drew him inside:

'You don't have a phone, mother', he explained. 'I decided I'd give you a surprise.'

Turning on the lights, a little anxious somehow, she led him further and further inside. He could hardly make out the stairs, the bookcase, the china cabinet, the dusty photo frames. The dog curled itself around his legs, whining softly:

'Down, Beauty', she shouted, threatening her with a kick. The bitch jumped aside, and she laughed. 'I only have to give her a warning, and she does what she's told. Poor old creature, she's almost completely blind. A mangy good-for-nothing really. All she can do is sleep, eat and shit, she's just waiting to die.'

'How old is she now?' he asked. For that was the best way of getting through to her: taking the back route, with these banal questions. The best way to get behind her sour manner, get past the purple flowers on her dressing-gown:

'I don't know, about fifteen.' Her voice had become so hoarse. 'You're supposed to multiply a dog's age by seven.'

He tilted his head deliberately, that was the way:

'About ninety-five then.'

She put his suitcase on a chair in the room. Then she screwed up her eyes again. And peered about her, as if she'd just woken up:

'What?'

'Beauty. If she were a person, she'd be ninety-five.' She laughed:

'Older than me, just think. Frighteningly old.' She closed the dressing-gown over her chest and held the collar with her hands. Covered in dark patches, he saw, like freckles (*se-nile pur-pu-ra*, he repeated to himself), some varnish on the short nails of her nicotine-stained fingers:

'Would you like a coffee?'

'If it's no trouble' – he knew that this was how he had to go about it, as she made her way masterfully through the kitchen, her domain. His hands in his pockets, he stood slouched in the doorway and looked around him.

Her back, so bent. She seemed to have slowed down, although she still had that same way of ceaselessly opening and closing the cupboard doors, laying out cups, spoons, napkins, making a lot of noise while he was forced to sit and watch. The kitchen walls, stained with grease. The little sliding window, with its broken pane. She'd put a sheet of newspaper over the glass. *Country sinks into chaos, disease and poverty*, he read. And he sat down on the broken plastic chair.

'It's nice and fresh', she said as she served the coffee. 'These days I can only get to sleep after I've had some coffee.'

'You shouldn't, mother. Coffee keeps you awake.' She shrugged her shoulders:

'To hell with that. With me it's always been the other way around.'

The yellow cup had a dark stain in the bottom, chips out of the rim. He stirred the coffee listlessly. Then, suddenly, as neither he nor she were saying anything, he wanted to run away – rewind the action as if watching a video – grab his suitcase, cross the room, the hallway, get beyond the stone path in the garden, out again into the little street of houses, almost all of them white. Get to a taxi, the airport, to another town, far from Passo da Guanxuma, to that other life from which he'd come. Anonymous, without ties, without a past. Forever, forever and ever. Until either of them died, he feared. And wished. Relief, shame:

'Go to bed', he suggested. 'It's very late, I shouldn't have come like this, without any warning. But you don't have a phone.'

She sat down opposite him, and her dressing-gown fell open. Between the purple flowers he saw the countless lines on her skin, crushed tissue paper. She screwed up her eyes, peering at his face as he took a sip of coffee:

'What's wrong?' she asked slowly. And that was the tone that set the opening for a new approach. But he coughed, and looked down at the diamond pattern of the table-cloth. Cold plastic, old strawberries:

'Nothing, mother. Nothing's wrong. I got homesick, that's all. Suddenly I got really homesick. For you, for everything.'

She took out a packet of cigarettes from her dressing-gown pocket:

'Give me a light, will you.'

He held out the lighter. She touched his hand awkwardly, her hands mottled with purple blotches against his very white hands. A wry sort of caress:

'Nice lighter.'

'It's French.'

'What's that inside.'

'Some liquid or other. Whatever it is that lighters have inside them. Except this one's transparent, you can't see it in the other ones.'

He held the lighter up against the light. Golden reflections, the green liquid sparkling. The dog crawled in under the table, whining softly. She seemed not to notice, entranced by what was behind the green, the golden liquid:

'It looks like the sea', she smiled. She tapped the cigarette against the rim of the cup, and handed the lighter back to him. 'So, young man, you came to visit me? Very good.'

He closed the lighter in his palm. Warm from her stained hand. 'Yes, mother. I got homesick.'

Hoarse laughter:

'Homesick? Do you know Elzinha hasn't been by for more than a month? I might die in here. Alone. God forbid. She'd only find out from the newspapers. If it got into the papers. Who cares about an old crock like me?' He lit a cigarette, and coughed heavily at the first drag:

'I live alone too, mother. If I died, no one would know. And it wouldn't get in the papers.'

She took a deep drag and blew some smoke rings. But she didn't follow them with her eyes. With the tip of her nail she was picking a chip off the rim of the cup:

'It's fate', she said. 'Your grandmother died alone. Your grandfather died alone. Your father died alone, remember? That weekend when I went to the beach. He was scared of the sea. It's a thing so big it frightens you, he'd say.' She flicked away the little chip of painted china. 'And not even a grandchild, he died without a grandchild. The thing he wanted most.'

'That's long past, mother. Forget it', he straightened his back, it was aching. No, he decided, not down into that abyss. The smell, a whole week, neighbours telephoning. He ran his fingertips over the faded diamonds on the tablecloth. 'I don't know how you can carry on living here alone, mother. This house is too big for just one person. Why don't you go and live with Elzinha?'

She pretended to spit to one side, with mock irony. That soap opera cynicism didn't go with the faded dressing gown, with the purple flowers, her near white hair, her nicotine-stained hands holding the cigarette smoked down to the butt:

'And put up with Pedro, with his delusions of grandeur? There'd have to be something really wrong with me, for God's sake. They'd hide me when they had visitors round, God forbid. The crazy old thing, the old witch. The old crone hidden away in the maid's room, like a black.' She tapped her cigarette. 'And as if that wasn't bad enough, do you think they'd let me take Beauty with me?'

Underneath the table, at the sound of her own name, the bitch whined more loudly:

'It's not really that bad, is it, mother? Elzinha's got her college. And deep down Pedro's a good person. It's just...'

She rummaged in the pockets of her dressing-gown and took out a pair of glasses; one lens cracked and the arms mended with sticky tape:

'Let me see you properly', she said. She adjusted the spectacles. He lowered his eyes. In the silence he sat listening to the ticking of the living-room clock. A tiny cockroach traced its path across the white tiles behind her:

'You look thinner', she observed. She seemed concerned. 'Much thinner.'

'It's my hair', he said. He ran his hand over his almost shaven head. 'And this three-day-old beard.'

'You've lost some hair, son.'

'It's my age. Almost forty.' He put out his cigarette, and coughed.

'And that rotten cough?'

'Cigarettes, mother. Air pollution.'

He raised his eyes, and for the first time looked straight into hers. Pale green behind the spectacle lenses, very alert all of a sudden. He thought of a line in a poem by Ana César; *It must be now, down this one-way street*. He almost said it. But she blinked first. She looked away under the table, carefully took hold of the mangy old dog and put it on her lap:

'But is everything alright?'

'Everything's fine, mother.'

'Work?'

He nodded. She stroked the dog's hairless ears. Then she looked straight at him again:

'What about your health? There are supposed to be some new bugs going around now, I saw it on the telly. Plagues.'

'I'm fine, thank God', he interrupted. He lit another

cigarette, his hands trembling a little. 'And Dona Alzira, still going strong?'

Holding the extinguished cigarette butt between her yellowed fingers, she leant back in the chair. Her eyes screwed up, as if she were looking right back through him. Into time and space. The dog rested its head on the table and shut its whitish eyes. She sighed and shrugged her shoulders:

'Poor woman. Even more decrepit than me.'

'You're not decrepit, mother.'

'That's what you think. There are times when I find I'm talking to myself. The other day, do you know who I was calling for the whole day long?' She waited for a little, he didn't say anything. 'Cândida, remember her? A good little girl, that one, even if she was just a black. But it was almost as though she was white. I was there calling her, calling her all day long. Cândida, hey, Cândida. Where've you got to, girl? Then I realised.'

'Cândida died, mother.'

She ran her hand over the dog's head again. More slowly this time. She closed her eyes, as if they were both sleeping. 'That's right, stabbed. Stuck like a pig, do you remember?' She opened her eyes. 'Do you want something to eat, son?'

'I ate on the plane.'

She pretended to spit again:

'Saints preserve us. Frozen food, God forbid. Like eating plastic. Remember the time I went on the plane?' He shook his head, she didn't notice. She was looking up, at the cigarette smoke losing itself against a ceiling stained by dampness, mould, time and solitude. 'I was so smart, I looked like a jet-setter. Going on the plane and everything, a real madame. With my vanity case, the sunglasses. You could tell people about it and no one would believe you.' She dunked a piece of bread in the cold coffee, and put it in the dog's almost toothless mouth. It swallowed it in one gulp. 'You know I liked the plane more than the city? It's so crazy, all that racket the whole time. It doesn't seem human, how do you stand it?'

'You get used to it, mother. You get to like it.'

'How's Beto?' she asked suddenly. And she gradually lowered her eyes until they were fixed right onto his again.

What if I were to lean over the precipice? he thought. What if I did it now, just like that. But instead he studied the tiles on the wall behind her. The cockroach had disappeared.

'He's there mother, living his life.'

She looked at the ceiling again:

'So thoughtful that Beto. He took me out to dinner, opened the car door for me. He was like something out of a movie. He pulled the chair out for me to sit down at the restaurant. No one's ever done that before.' She squinted at him. 'What was the name of that restaurant again? Some foreign name.'

'*Casserole*, mother. *La Casserole*.' He almost smiled, he had a little boy's eyes, he remembered. 'It was nice, that evening, wasn't it?'

'Yes', she agreed. 'So nice, it was just like a movie.' She stretched her hand out across the table, almost touching his. He spread his fingers, with a kind of longing. So sad, so sad. Then she pulled back, dropping her fingers onto the bitch's hairless head:

'Beto liked you, mother. He liked you a lot' – he drew his fingers together again. Then he ran them over the hairs on his arm. Memories, distances: 'He said you were very chic, mother.'

'Chic, me? A common, decrepit old woman.' She laughed, vainly, her stained hand on her white hair. She sighed. 'So handsome. Such a nice boy, that's what I call a nice boy. I said it to Elzinha, right in front of Pedro, to have a bit of a dig at him. I said it out loud, just like that. If someone's not well bred, you can see it right away in their face. There's no point in putting on appearances, it's written in the stars. Just like Beto, with those torn trousers. Who'd ever have thought he was such a nice boy, wearing those trainers?' She looked into his eyes again. 'That's a real friend you've got there, son. A bit like you even, I thought to myself. They look like brothers. The same height, the same manner, they really do look just like brothers.'

'We haven't seen each other for quite a while, mother.'

She leaned over a little, squeezing the bitch's head against the table. Beauty opened her whitish eyes. Although she was blind, she too seemed to be looking at him. They sat there looking at each other like this. For an almost unbearable length of time, amidst the cigarette smoke, the overflowing ashtrays, the empty cups, the three of them, himself, his mother and Beauty:

'But why?'

'Mother', he began. His voice trembled. 'Mother, it's so difficult', he repeated. And said nothing more.

It was then that she got up. Suddenly, throwing the bitch onto the floor like a dirty rag. She began to gather up cups, spoons, ashtrays and throw them all into the sink. After piling up the dishes, squirting on some washing-up liquid and turning on the taps, she walked to and fro while he sat there looking at her, so bent, a little older, her hair turned almost completely white, her voice a little hoarser, her fingers yellower and yellower from smoking. She put her glasses away in her dressing-gown and buttoned the collar, looking at him like someone who wants to change the subject – and that was a sign for him to try another approach, the right one this time – she said,

'Your room's just as it was, upstairs. I'm going to bed because I've got the market first thing tomorrow. There are clean sheets in the bathroom cupboard.'

Then she did something that she wouldn't have done before. She took hold of him by his ears to kiss him, not on the forehead, but on both cheeks. Almost lingeringly. That smell: cigarettes, onions, dog, soap and old age. And something else besides, something moist that seemed like pity, a weariness from having seen too much. Or love. A kind of love:

'Tomorrow we'll talk properly, mother. There's plenty of time, sleep well.'

Leaning across the table, he lit another cigarette and listened to her treading heavily up the stairs to the first floor. When he heard the door of the room slam, he got up and left the kitchen.

He took a few giddy steps across the room. The huge dark wooden table. Eight places, all empty. He stopped in front of his grandfather's picture – a slightly lopsided face with his mother's green watery eyes, eyes that he too had inherited. That man, he thought, died in the middle of the countryside, alone with a revolver and his fate. He put his hand in the inside pocket of his jacket, took out the little bottle with its foreign label and drank. When he took it away, drops of whisky rolled down the corners of his mouth, down his neck and shirt, onto the floor. The dog licked the worn carpet, its eyes almost blind, its tongue feeling about in search of the liquid.

He opened his eyes. He found himself staring at the big living-room mirror. In the depths of this mirror that hung on the living-room wall of an old house in a provincial town, he could make out the shadow of a painfully thin man, his head almost shaved, with the startled eyes of a child. He put the bottle on the table and took off his jacket. He was sweating heavily. He slung the jacket over the back of a chair and began to unbutton his shirt, stained with whisky and sweat.

One by one, he undid the buttons. He turned on the lamp, so that the room would be lighter and, with his shirt off, began to stroke the purple marks, the same colour as the stair carpet had once been – what colour was it now? – that spread beneath the hairs on his chest. With his fingertips he touched the right-hand side of his neck, tilting his head as if feeling for a seed in the dark. Then he slumped to his knees. God, he thought, and stretched out his other hand to touch the near-blind dog, its coat dappled with pink patches. The same as those on the worn stair-carpet, the same as those on the skin of his chest, beneath the hair. Curly, dark, soft:

'Beauty', he whispered. 'Beauty, you're such a beauty, Beauty.'

II
The Leaves of Fate Have Fallen

'There's pain, there's love, there's love and pain: a man imagines the shape of his future, and asks bewildered: which way from here?'

(Adélia Prado: *The Intrepid Heart*)

Venus

Six years ago, he was crazy about her. Completely crazy about her. And the problem was – one of the problems, there were others, much more serious ones – problem number one, if you like, was that it was all happening too soon. When you're twenty or thirty, six years of passion can be a long (or for that matter, a short) time. But, as it happened, he was only twelve. And she was a year older. They were both at that halfway stage when it was too soon for some things, and too late for most of the others.

She was called Beatriz. His name doesn't matter. But it wasn't quite Dante, not quite yet. Years later, he'd try to remember How It All Began. But couldn't. Of course he couldn't. Confused scenes were all he'd recall; jumbled up and out of their chronological order, making it impossible for him to work out the before and the after of that moment when he fell so madly in love with Beatriz.

There were two scenes that came back most often. The first one was at a birthday party, but he couldn't say whose. One of those summer parties where all the windows in the house are flung open, letting in a strong, clear light which, later on, as it gradually faded, stained the evening sky crimson. He remembered a glass of guaraná, his mother's velvet skirt – he always used to cling to his mother at parties, peeping at the others, the ones his own age, from a distance. He remembered the glass of guaraná, the velvet skirt (would it have been moss green?) and the gas-filled balloon he was holding. Then his mother suddenly asked him who he thought was the prettiest girl at the party. Without needing to think, he answered,

'Beatriz.'

His mother laughed and threw back her hair – golden hair, gold as the guaraná, gold as the summer light – and said,

'Goodness, that little starlet?'

Years later, he'd be unable to find the meaning of the word *starlet* in the dictionary. But back then, with the balloon in one hand, the guaraná in the other, his elbows digging into the velvet (would it have been navy-blue?) of his mother's skirt, the first thing he thought of was a star. Perhaps it was because of the way his mother's hair moved and everything sparkled that he thought of a star. A little star. A skinny, kind of nervous little star. Beatriz had a long ballerina's neck which made her taller than the other girls, and a lovely way of sparkling when she moved her plumb-straight back, looking about her like a grown-up woman.

Starlet starlet starlet starlet – he said it again and again until the word lost its meaning and, ground down to a spark, it flew off with the balloon which he released from his hiding-place behind the bamboo thicket. The sun was just disappearing and the first star had come out. The Evening Star, Vesper, Venus, so people said. People said a lot of things he didn't understand yet.

Scenes

The other scene must have been at one of those end-of-term primary school galas in the Southern Cross Cinema.

He'd be sitting in the stalls, because he couldn't sing or dance or recite or do anything the others could sit and watch and clap – as he was sitting and watching and clapping now. Then Beatriz would come out onto the stage wearing a white bouffant dress and sit down on a chair, while the teacher-compère would position an accordion in her arms. Although tall for her age, Beatriz almost disappeared from the stage behind that enormous accordion – all you could see was her pale, serious face; her straight fringe peeking out above the instrument; and her long legs below it – so thin that her lace socks sagged down over the buckles of her black patent leather shoes. Her two hands, nails heavily bitten, lay on the keys.

Then it would happen. From memory, years later, he had the impression that there was a silence just before she began. A silence that came before the sparkle. Maybe not, maybe he just imagined it.

Suddenly, just after this uncertain silence, Beatriz's fingers with their chewed nails would begin to move over the keys. Gradually a little waltz called *The Leaves of Fate Have Fallen* began to emerge from the accordion and her voice started to flow, a voice that was thin and fine like glass, like a needle, like a thorn. Our-love-spelled-tenderness-and-bliss-divine, he remembered, unrivalled-joy-one-day-you-were-almost-mine. His heart beat faster. As it had when he'd released the balloon late in the afternoon, behind the bamboo thicket. And something sparkled in the vermilion evening air, within the flaking walls of the Southern Cross Cinema. That was all there was, just scenes.

After that one, others.

More ordinary scenes, with him almost always sitting

behind or next to her in the first, second, third, fourth and fifth forms of primary school. He'd copy from Beatriz in Arithmetic. She'd copy from him in Portuguese. They both got good marks. But every month they got the lowest possible mark for Behaviour because they never stopped talking. Every morning, except Saturday and Sunday.

On Saturdays there was no Beatriz. But occasionally on Sundays, at ten o'clock mass, she would appear again, at her mother's side. Dona Lucy didn't wear velvet skirts nor did she have golden hair. She was a widow and dressed in black, her hair in a bun, a rosary in her hand. In her company Beatriz's sparkle disappeared, dimmed by a pain which she or he would only have been able to understand later, if they had had enough time. But they didn't.

The Separation

Suddenly – or not suddenly, but so gradually with every day just like every other day, it was as if it happened suddenly, in the blinking of an eye, in the turning of a page – a lot of time went by. Then, when they started high school, it happened. The Separation. He went to the State school, she went to the Convent school. After the long holidays one summer, there was no more Beatriz in the mornings.

But on Sundays she would be at the four o'clock matinée. And no Dona Lucy. Now she was surrounded by Betinha, Aureluce, Tanara and her other rowdy girlfriends, a whole row of them in the Southern Cross cinema. With their Banlon blouses and giggling, their popcorn and the rustling of sweet papers being screwed up just as Johnny Weissmuller was about to fall into the hands of the pygmy cannibals. Quicksands and headhunters, poisoned spears. He hated all those little girlies and their shrieking and squealing. Except for her. When he hung back or speeded up so as to meet her at the exit he'd blush a bit, say *hi-ya!* – and rush away quickly. At those moments he'd carry her off inside him, forgiving everything.

She was growing, but not like the other girls, in front and behind; mostly Beatriz was growing upwards. Her neck was getting longer and longer, her silky-smooth black ponytail would bounce against her back, just under the shoulders. He wasn't. He wasn't growing in any direction at all. Only, it seemed, inside. He had this awful sense of something thick and grubby clogging him up inside. His movements were becoming disjointed and his voice was cracking. Pimples and hairs were turning up in unexpected places. He felt heavy, sluggish, uncomfortable, as if he didn't fit his own body, as if he were suspended between having lost an old way of controlling himself and not having found the new way. There had to be one.

It was about then that the rumours started. That girl of Lucy's, people would say, but immediately change the subject when he came along. How awful, he could still hear them, what a tragedy. First the husband and now the daughter. Poor little thing, not even fifteen yet. He learnt how to listen without being seen, in the shadows, behind doors.

Until one day he snared the new word: *leukaemia*. He found it in the dictionary. But he couldn't quite grasp what it meant. Blood cells. *Globulos*, that sounded nice, sort of round. Sounded like 'lobe', 'lobelia', 'bauble': glo-bulo. White, in excess. Does it kill you, he asked at school. They said it did. Rapidly.

No Time to Lose

Then came the rush.

There wasn't a day to lose, for although it was still very early, he also began to suspect that it was already much too late. He looked for Betinha, a note all ready, written with a Parker 51 on proper notepaper. *I want to talk to you tomorrow without fail, see you in the square, after class:*

'You know then do you?' asked Betinha, looking him straight in the eye.

He said yes, he did.

Late that afternoon the reply came back: Beatriz agreed. Tomorrow in the square, without fail:

'You're sure you know?' asked Betinha again.

Again he said yes, he did. He asked if it was true.

Betinha nodded, it was. Before she went, she added,

'Take a good look at her neck. She's got some lumps here, like this, all swollen up. That's the disease.'

He did take a good look, just about noon the next day, as they sat on a bench in the middle of the square, as he asked, trembling with love:

'Beatriz, I want to be your boyfriend.'

She pressed a book, History of Brazil, to her breast:

'You're just a kid', she said.

He could hardly bear to look at her. He looked at the coloured lozenges of paving-stone in the middle of the square. They made circles, squares, big stars and little ones; some even smaller, starlets:

'But if I'm a kid', he began to say slowly, persuasively, 'If I'm a kid, then so are you, because you're only twelve.'

'Thirteen', she corrected him. And she lifted her face towards the noonday sun. The swollen ganglions almost disappeared like that. *Gan-gli-ons*, he repeated to himself, this word he barely knew.

He was startled to realise that Beatriz was wearing lipstick. A very pale lipstick, hardly noticeable. She seemed so gay and so distant that the thick grubby thing inside him began squirming as if it wanted to get out. A snake preparing to strike, vomit gathered in its throat. He was still trying to control it when he insisted,

'But I love you, Beatriz. I really love you. I love you so much.'

'Well I don't love you', she lowered her eyes, trying to meet his. When she did, she spoke almost with a smile, like someone offering something sweet, not like someone sticking in a sharpened knife, 'I just like you as a friend.'

'If it's just friends I'm not interested', he said plaintively.

It must have been March because the sun was so hot that it was causing beads of sweat to run down his face, between the pimples, to his upper lip, where those dark hairs were beginning to thicken. His pubescent male face must have looked loathsome, bestial. Later, much later, if they'd asked him, although no one would ever know about it, he could say it hadn't been his fault. It was that filthy thing inside him rising uncontrollably to his gorge, passing his tongue and teeth to shape itself into the cruel question which he hurled out into the warm midday air (and the Sun was at the Equinox, it must have been predestined):

'Beatriz, do you know you're going to die?'

She got up. Neither pale, nor tearful. Remote, fateful. He got up too. Only then did he notice that, besides the lipstick, she was wearing high-heeled shoes which made her about a foot taller than him. Behind her he could see the church tower. Maybe one or two palm trees. The water tower in the distance, very high up. The bell began to ring. Beatriz turned her back and walked off, neck erect, the history book pressed to her uplifted breasts which, he realised, appeared uplifted because – and this was the final blow – in addition to the lipstick and heels, Beatriz was also wearing a bra.

Beatriz was a woman. And she was going to die.

The Departure

Come back, he wanted to say, standing there in the middle of the square.

But now, so many years later, he couldn't tell whether he really did want to call out, there, at midday on a Pisces afternoon, or whether it was later that he softly repeated it, at night alone in bed, in the same room as his elder brother, that night or all the nights afterwards as the summer drew further away and the nights grew colder and colder, through June, July and August, wrapped up in blankets, repeating his whole life through: Beatriz, come back and I'll look after you and find a way to make you better and then we can go away to Africa or the Pacific or Eurasia or some other place where you can get completely well by my side and forever, come back and I'll look after you and I won't ever let you die.

He didn't say anything. Treading slowly, looking up at the sun, Beatriz went out of his twelve-year-old life forever.

Oh, Babe...

A little more time passed. One, two years during which, as well as growing inside, he began to grow just like everyone else – in all directions. Those fine hairs above his lip thickened, others appeared and darkened into their proper curves and curls. His pimples disappeared, his voice settled down. That filthy stuff inside him turned into a kind of thick milk which he discovered how to draw out by means of movements of his hand and shudders of his body. In the next bed, Toninho used to say,

'You'll get hairs on the palm of your hand. You'll get TB doing that. If you want, tell me one day and I'll take you down to the red-light district. Or go on your own, find La

Morocha's place and say you're my brother, she knows the score.'

It was during those years that Beatriz went away. To the capital for treatment they said.

That was after a period in which she exchanged that light pink lipstick for another, very bright red one, and those low heels for some other really high ones, and plunging necklines, bare shoulders, short skirts, legs crossed at the club, shrill laughter in the street, cigarettes and rouge on her ever-whiter cheeks. Beatriz passed from hand to hand. Through Cacá's hands, Cacá who in Physical Education classes would drop his pants to show off his prick, the biggest in the school, to anyone who wanted to see it. Or hold it, some even held it. Through Mauro's hands, Mauro who had hairs on his chest and could put away a basketball like nobody's business. And Luizão and Pancho and Caramujo and Bira and so many others that he couldn't even remember their names or faces properly; people were spreading it around the street-corners, the snooker halls, the square or the matinée show, she'll do the lot, just go up to her and put your hand on her there, she gives it to everybody – she's a real slag.

Hardly anything happened to him, apart from a disastrous attempt to go out with Betinha, after Beatriz went away. But he just asked about her, until one day Betinha got fed up and started going out with Luizão, who had a Lambretta. Virtually nothing apart from that body growing in unexpected directions and a gothic *B* drawn in fond secrecy in the end pages of his exercise books, especially in the Geography ones, when he was trying to memorise capital cities – Switzerland, capital Berne; Poland, capital Warsaw; Honduras, capital Te-gu-ci-galpa – and at every strange name he'd say again and again, dying with longing, shall we go there then Beatriz, who knows – shall we?

He learnt how to drive his father's red-upholstered white Simca Chambord. But you soon got out of Passo da

Guanxuma: it petered out into just four red and dusty dirt roads, stretching to the horizon. He had to have a private Maths teacher. He had to repeat the second year of Latin, and couldn't get past the first declension: terra, terrae, terram. He wrote sonnets which didn't scan, and listened endlessly to a single of Silvinha Telles singing Oh-Babe-if-you-knew-how-much-I-love-you-the-world-would-be-sweet-Babe-sweet...

Until that day.

Mars

It was always summer when something happened. Perhaps because in the summer people would bring their chairs outside into the street and sit along the pavements, look up at the stars and talk about everything that they didn't usually talk about during the day. He'd learnt how to blend into the shadows without being noticed. He'd become a shadow on the lookout for something never clearly expressed; on the edge of that instant when there'd be no more secrets to discover and life would become raw and tangible because he'd touched it himself, not just heard about it.

He stood there listening, as word followed word:

'Did you hear about Lucy's girl?'

'Who, Beatriz?'

'Well, dearie, has Lucy got any other daughters?'

'I only asked. What's happened to her?'

'Well, they say she died, in Porto Alegre.'

'You don't say, dear. When?'

'Yesterday, or the day before yesterday or the day before that. I'm not sure exactly. They're burying her down there.'

'How awful. So young.'

'Yes. What a waste. She wasn't even sixteen.'

'A pretty kid. A bit headstrong, but with her heart in the right place.'

'Apparently she died pregnant.'
'Dear God, you don't say.'
'And she knew she was going to die. It just tore her apart and she hit rock bottom.'
'But who was the father?'
'God knows. She was gadding about with everyone here in Passo. Zulma's Cacá, Lia's Luizão, Otaviano's boy Bira. Not to mention the ones down there, God knows how many.'
'What a crazy business.'
'Apparently her head split right open before she died.'
'How do you mean, split right open?'
'Well, it split open, ugh! Just like a gourd in the sun. That, you know... disease.'
'But poor Lucy. First her husband, then the daughter.'
'We've all got our cross to bear.'
'Poor Beatriz.'
'God rest her soul.'
'Hey, wasn't your boy sweet on her?'

Was he? (It's so long ago now, the bottle of wine's almost empty and Marianne Faithfull's embittered voice sings *As Tears Go By*, and there have been so many new and unexpected pains, if only he could have known then, at that moment, with those lost young eyes he had then.) Had he really been, such a crude expression, *sweet on Beatriz?* He couldn't really say.

He must have looked up and seen the red star (Mars, would it have been?) which shone that summer right above La Morocha's place. He had an urge, he had a thudding in his chest and sweat on his brow. But he waited for the subject to change and sprawled across the living-room sofa, he turned the pages of the local paper *The Southern Cross*. David Nasser, flying saucers, Marcia and Maristela, the navvies building Brasilia, Odete Lara, things like that. Only after hanging around the house for hours – once again with that thick stuff, that filthy stuff, that frenzied stuff churning inside him – did he decide to emerge ever so slowly from the shadows into the light that shone from the lamppost onto the people sitting on the pavement.

And like that, in the light from the lamp-post, from cigarettes, fireflies and stars, with his shirt open at the chest and both hands sunk deep into his pockets, he looked so sure of himself and so determined that no one could have had the courage to refuse him anything at all when he asked,

'Will you lend me the car, Dad?'

Dust

He got going and took off up the hill roads towards La Morocha's place. Way up there.

'*El hermano de Tonico?*' she asked, offering him the cup of fresh maté, with a glint of her gold front tooth. 'So that's what you look like. He told me about you, but still, what a cutie.'

Her rings glittered as she opened the door for him to make his way into the smoky interior. There they were already, or they'd arrive later, he couldn't remember: Caramujo, Pancho, Bira and maybe another one or two out of all those scum who'd got at Beatriz. He didn't speak to anyone. He sat down by himself at a table, asked for a pack of Hudson filters and a beer. Before he could order his second one, an ageing blonde, with green eyes and a missing tooth, asked if he'd mind if she sat with him. She was wearing a tight brightly coloured velvet skirt, he never again managed to remember the exact colour, although he was certain that it was neither moss green nor navy blue.

The following morning when, with a lot of yelling, Toninho finally managed to wake him up, all he could remember was having asked to hear *The Leaves of Fate Have Fallen*, after throwing up spectacularly in the middle of the room. And more than anything else, the gaping legs of an ageing blonde on a bed with strange smelling sheets. Nothing else, just an opaque mist and the taste of straw in his mouth.

Today, so many years later – his brain cells blasted by alcohol, drugs, insomnia, rejections, and his memory playing tricks on him – when he focuses his attention completely on that barren core within something that was once dense, but which has gradually dispersed; all that time and those feelings swept away like dust. No matter how hard he tries: the small hours, the family home, the silent phone, he remembers almost nothing apart from what has been said here tentatively about Beatriz or himself or what he now calls, with fondness and bitterness, *Those Days*.

It was all a long, long time ago, they go on telling him, forget it. They still say things he doesn't understand.

III

On the Shore of the Open Sea

And once again you come to me and speak of the open sea which lies off the shores of your country, and of the icy wind blowing down from the Pole in winter when there is no bay, when no gull or albatross skims or dives over the grey water as they did before, hooking fish with their razor beaks; but the waters I remember were bright and green, the sun shone and I believe the bird's beak flashed silver as it entered those waters; the waters you speak of when you lead me on endless walks, into stories where there is no greenness or brightness and cloud shields the sun, where I imagine you standing alone on an endless strip of sand, the wind lashing your face, your fingers blue with cold, sunk deep into your pockets; the wind lashing your face, the same face that looks at me strangely now, your lashing gaze deflected by the knives and stones in my pupils, your face is more naked than ever at the sea's edge, with that wind lashing, stirring your hair and your thoughts, I don't know what stirs me now as your gaze once again slips far away from mine, from your wide brow where you sometimes brush back your hair with both hands, in a mixture of undisguised indolence and sensuality, and when your eye drifts away like that, I don't know where, maybe to your home of yesterday by the open sea, which I cannot reach, just as you elude me now, but it's in the moments when the stones and knives deep in my eye drive away your gaze that I examine you in minute detail, you'll never realise how intimately I know every millimetre of your skin, the steep arch of your eyebrows before they thin to nothing, that spot where you usually shave badly, I know too those secret tufts of stiff hair hidden below your lower lip, and I watch you so surreptitiously that you never notice me, as I take in every hair, every pore in search of that innermost something you obstinately hide from me, masked by stories like that one about the sea, old aunts, initiations, exiles, imprisonments, scars; I suppose you think that it's your way of giving yourself to me but I am stung by the realisation that your stories conceal even more, as if by telling me about yourself you were denying the possibility of my discovering what there is of you behind such tales and so I try to hide from them as they entangle me ever more deeply in what you are not, your past; I try to run far away, every night, like a child afraid of sin and the punishments inflicted by vengeful angels with flaming swords, I promise myself never again to listen, never again to hold you to me so deceptively close, and I suddenly run off so that you'll see I can scarcely bear your presence, poison poison, sometimes I say harsh things, I want to make you understand that it's not like that, that I am more afraid than I have ever felt in all these months, and there's nothing for it, I always, always come back, to be trapped again in the same game and although I think I know the rules, I allow myself to be deceived by your strange liturgies, making my pact with your indecipherable fears, accepting your discarded crumbs like a hungry dog grateful for a meatless bone; I always return, saddened by your eye which descends upon mine as upon no other, fearing the knife, the stone, the blade of your long stories, your sad memories; full of damp corridors, old maids locked in their rooms, balconies looking out onto narrow streets where unmarried girls are drying their hair and coyly displaying themselves, I shall always come back because I need that bone, those crumbs which have sustained me all this time, and I always weep when the days end because I know we will not seek each other at night, when the danger mounts and unable to contain myself, I want to attack you like a vampire, bleed you dry and leave you dumb, without any stories to hide behind, to sink my teeth into in your throat and rip out the life which you always discreetly deny me, but when you don't come no one knows that I am left standing like an old man in the last patch of winter sun, dimmed by your absence, yet in your presence once more I am cast into such deep depression as you tear me apart, leading me astray along these familiar paths where behind every word I desperately try to find some meaning, code or sign which might let me hope for a byway in which to linger, a place where you will not glance away so soon, where your finger will not brush my arm so fleetingly, where you will dwell a while longer over me and, rather than treat me like a pit in which to vomit up your undigested bitterness, think that you might accept my games too, those games, the leftovers that I never wanted; but this is all futile and I know only too well how I have tried to feed off that filthy crust which we hungrily and sorrowfully call our little-hopes-and-dreams, while I waste away like an animal fed on meagre water alone, and standing here beside you, unseen by you, I slowly sharpen the stones and knives and train myself in the use of blades so that the night won't find me sleepless again, and alone, reassembling your features one by one; now, when those dark eyes of yours, tranquil like the waters of the winter ocean on the shore where perhaps you still walk, gaze into mine you will be torn apart and crawling across this floor we litter every day with scribbled bits of paper and cigarette-ends, bleeding and moaning, you will beg me for that very gesture which you never gave but which might wrench us once and for all out of that sweet lie into which maybe we have been gradually sinking – drunk like flies on sugar, sticky with our own cowed and cynical sweetness, contaminated by our false purity, drenched with words and literature – the gesture might throw us absolutely naked, stripped of all stories, stripped of all words, onto that same sea shore on the coast of your country; and again you come to me and reach me and invade me and take me and beg me and lose me and flood over me with your ever elusive eyes and you open your mouth to unleash new stories and so again I'm made whole and without pressure, and I concentrate on the things you tell me, and silent, subdued, I contemplate you as you stab me exquisitely, making it clear in each never-to-be-kept promise that I must not expect anything but that coloured mask; that this is how you want me because this is how you are and you only want me like this and you use me every day, and we honestly use one another like this, with me hungrily digesting what your body rejects, drinking your magical filthy poison and step by step I sink into that pit which, for all I know, is our great knowledge of each other (or our great deception); at dusk we separate cautiously and each back to our own solitude, where we will slowly weave our next lie, spun so fine that the next morning it will be like pure truth and we'll smile affably, averting our eyes, the same as ever, as the day moves on, building up millimetre by millimetre a harmony which will only be threatened by each fearful brushing of eyes or skin, the ice, the worms gnawing away at the vaults which we insist on guarding inviolate, until the not-done that has accumulated during this time grows like a cancerous cell and explodes into open sores and haemorrhages, crazy red flowers on the surface of our skin; we refuse to touch them out of disgust or cowardice or a passion so possessed that it couldn't endure the holy water of its own baptism, and as you talk and ensnare me and envelop me and fascinate me with your strange accent and your low assonant voice, I still imagine that the sea is not that dense dark sea you speak to me about – without palm trees, islands, bays or seagulls – but a different sea, brighter and greener, in a land where it is always summer and emotions are clean like the sand on which we tread; you don't know about this sea of mine because I tell you nothing, I fear it will turn out to be that pitiful, hungry thing again, those little-hopes-and-fears, but when I turn my gaze away from yours, I still keep your face inside me and I know, whether by choice or destiny, that it doesn't matter which; we are so entangled that it would be impossible to retreat, we must go to the end of this thing which I have never experienced before, or maybe I invented it just to pass the time on those days when nothing seems to happen and maybe I invented us both as playthings to help the mornings and afternoons pass without this desolate search for a reason, a reason for traumas and sleepless nights and futile moments spent eagerly waiting and night-time imaginings, and slowly you speak, and slowly I fall silent, and slowly I accept, and slowly I break, and slowly I fall apart, and slowly I fall deeper and deeper and now I can't get back to the surface because the hand which you've stretched out to me pushes me down further and further, and you repeat those long sad crazy stories, like this one which would end here, now, like this, if only you didn't come and blind me and drown me in an open sea that we know should not end like this, not here, not now....

IV
Blues Without Ana

When Ana left me – that sentence has stuck in my mind in two ways – and after Ana left me. I know it's not a proper sentence, just the beginning of one, but that was what stuck in my mind. That's how I thought of it, *when Ana left me*, and that discontinuity was the only kind of continuity there was. Between that *when* and that *after*, there was nothing else in my mind or my life apart from the blankness left by Ana's absence, although I could have filled it up – that blankness without Ana – in lots of ways, as many as you like, with words or with actions, or with non-words and inaction, because silence and immobility were two of the least painful ways I found in that period to fill my days, my flat, my bed, my walks, my dinners, my thoughts, my fucks and all those other things which make up a life with/without someone like Ana inside it.

When Ana left me, I stood for a long time in the living room of the apartment with her note in my hands. It was around eight o'clock in the evening. The clocks were on summer time and through the open living-room window it was still possible to make out, in that eight o'clock in the evening light, a few traces of gold and red left by the sun going down behind the buildings over towards Pinheiros. I stood there a long time, in the middle of the living room, Ana's last note in my hands, looking out of the window at the reds and golds in the sky. And I remember thinking, 'now the phone's going to ring': it might have been Lucinha ringing from the agency or Paulo from the film club or Nelson from Paris or my mother from the South, inviting me to dinner, to snort some coke, to see Nastassia Kinski in the nude, asking what the weather was like or something like that, but it didn't ring so after some time in which it hadn't rung I thought, 'now someone's going to ring the doorbell': It might be the janitor delivering some mail, the neighbour from upstairs looking for her Persian cat that liked to escape down the stairs, or even one of those nasty little kids you get in apartment blocks who love ringing other people's doorbells and then running away, or simply a mistake, maybe. But the doorbell didn't ring either, and I stood there for a good while longer without any means of salvation, in the middle of the room which was beginning to turn a bluish colour as the evening drew on, like the inside of a fish tank, Ana's note in my hands, doing absolutely nothing except breathe.

After Ana left me – not at that exact moment I'm actually standing here, because that moment is the moment-when, not the moment-after, and nothing takes place in the moment-when, just Ana's absence, like a round, shining soap bubble suspended in space, right in the middle of the living room, and I'm standing inside that bubble too, suspended too, but not shining, quite the opposite, opaque, dim, dull and still dressed in one of the suits I wear to work, just the knot of my tie slightly loosened, because it's the beginning of summer and the sweat running over my body is beginning to moisten my hands and dissolve the ink on the letters of Ana's note – after Ana left me, as I was saying, I took to the bottle, as per usual.

From all the days that followed, my mouth remembers just three tastes: vodka, tears and coffee. The taste of vodka, without water or lemon or orange juice, straight vodka, transparent, slightly viscous, those nights when I'd arrive home and, without Ana, I'd sit on the sofa and drink out of the sole crystal glass to survive a row we'd had. The taste of tears would come in the small hours when I'd manage to crawl from the living room into the bedroom and throw myself onto the double bed, without Ana, I didn't change the sheets for the longest time because they still held her smell, and then I'd hit myself and groan and claw at the walls, hug the pillows as if they were her body, and weep and weep and weep until I fell into a dreamless leaden sleep. The taste of sugarless coffee followed me through the hangover mornings and afternoons in the agency, amongst ad copy and jumping every time the phone rang. Mixed in with the dregs of the taste of vodka, tears and coffee, the thumping in my head, the sick feeling in the pit of my stomach and my puffy eyes, especially on Fridays, just before those Saturdays and Sundays without Ana ever again came crashing down on me, there would come the certainty that suddenly, normal as anything, someone would say 'telephone-call-for-you' and from the other end of the line that familiar voice would say, 'I-miss-you-I-want-to-come-back'. It never happened.

What did begin to happen, halfway through that cycle of tastes: vodka, tears and coffee, was that I got a taste of vomit in my mouth as well. Because halfway between the vodka and the tears, when I crawled from the living room into the bedroom, sometimes the little corridor of the apartment would seem as huge as an ocean liner's at the height of a storm. Between the living room and the bedroom, at the height of the storm, swaying inside the ocean liner, I couldn't help stopping at the bathroom door, in the little corridor that seemed so big. I would kneel down on the floor, put my arms very carefully around the yellow porcelain lavatory bowl, as though I were embracing Ana's still-present body, prudently put my round specs with the red frames away in my pocket, and slowly stick my index finger deeper and deeper down my throat, until almost all the vodka, along with the remains of any sandwiches I'd eaten during the day – I could hardly swallow anything else then – mingled with the taste of all the cigarettes I'd smoked, poured out of my mouth into the yellow porcelain lavatory bowl which was not Ana's body. I would vomit and vomit in the early morning, abandoned in the middle of the wilderness like a saint whom God has left to do penance – and all I could ask was why, why, why, my God, have you forsaken me? I never did get an answer.

Some time after those days that I can't really remember – neither what they were like or how many there were, for all that remained was the taste of vodka, tears and coffee and sometimes vomit too, mixed, towards the end of that phase, with the taste of the pizzas I would order by phone, mainly at weekends, and which would still be there on Saturday, Sunday and Monday mornings abandoned on the living-room table, along with stuffed ashtrays and napkins with phrases I couldn't decipher that I'd written the previous night, and which were probably inanities like come-back-to-me-Ana or I-can't-live-without-you, words half dissolved by wine stains and the grease from the pizzas. After those days there began the time when I wanted to kill the Ana inside everything that had connected us, which included that bed, that bedroom, that living-room, that table, that apartment, the life that had become mine after Ana left me.

I sent the pale green sheets that still had Ana's smell to the laundry – it would have been too cruel for me now to remember that smell again, that smell right in the curve where the neck becomes the shoulder, a place where no one person's smell is the same as another's, I moved the furniture around, bought some pieces by Kutka and Gregório, a microwave oven, blank video tapes, two dozen crystal glasses, and began to bring other women home. Women who were not Ana, women who could never be Ana, women who weren't and wouldn't ever be anything like Ana. If Ana had small, firm breasts, I would choose them for their large, soft breasts, if Ana had ash blonde hair, I would bring back ones with dark hair, if Ana's voice was husky, I would choose them for their shrill voices which moaned coarse things when we were screwing, quite different from the things which Ana said or didn't say, she never said anything apart from darling-darling or my-dear-little-baby, running the fingers of her right hand over my neck and the fingers of her left hand over my back. Gina came over, the one with the black knickers, and Lilian, the one with the cold green eyes, and Beth, with the plump thighs and icy feet, and Marilene, who smoked too much and had a son, and Mariko, the second-generation Japanese who wanted to be blonde, and Marta, Luiza, Creuza, Júlia, Deborah, Vivian, Paula, Teresa, Luciana, Solange, Maristela, Adriana, Vera, Silvia, Neusa, Denise, Karina, Cristina, Márcia, Nadir, Aline too and more than fifteen Marias, and one by one all the tarty little darlings from Augusta Street, with their white boots and leather miniskirts, and the girls who advertise 'extras' in the newspapers. I think I've been here once before, one of them would say, and I'd say I don't remember, maybe. Waiting while she took off her clothes, drinking a bit more before trying to enter her; my prick almost never obeying my command, I'd bury my head in her breasts and dribbling would snivel, you know, since Ana left me I haven't ever been able to do it. Even when my prick eventually did obey, after I'd managed to come burning and dry inside her, wiped myself off with a towel and thrown her out with a cheque – then I'd fling myself face down on the bed and beg Ana's forgiveness for betraying her like that, with those tramps. Betraying Ana (who had deserted me) hurt more than her desertion but I still went down in that shipwreck every night, in the huge corridor on the ocean liner in that apartment at the height of the storm and without a life jacket.

After Ana left me, many months later, there came the round of spirit messages, of I Ching, of conch shells, Tarot cards, pendulums, séances, numbers and candomblé offerings – she'll come back, they guaranteed it, but she didn't.

Then came the round of group therapy, psychodrama, Jungian dream workshops, transactional analysis, and after that the rounds of piety, with offerings to Saint Anthony, seven-day candles, novenas for Saint Rita, donations to poor little children and helpless old people. And then the round of new haircuts, new frames for my glasses, a younger wardrobe, *Zoomp, Mr. Wonderful*, body building, stretch exercises, Yoga, swimming, Tai Chi, dumbbells, jogging, and I started to become so handsome, restored, and feeling I'd really got over it, and that I was free and I'd forgotten the time before Ana had left me. Then I allowed myself the round of weekends in Búzios, Guarujá or Monte Verde, and suddenly maybe Carla, Vicente's wife, so understanding and mature, and unexpectedly Mariana, Vicente's sister, so compliant and natural in her metallic dental floss bikini and, why not, eventually Vicente himself, so attentive in the way he'd put ice cubes in my Scotch or take me on another good-hearted run across the ice rink, lightly resting his muscular thigh tanned by windsurfing and sun on my muscular thigh, likewise tanned by windsurfing and sun. So much time went by after Ana left me and I survived; the world gradually became a huge fan spread out to reveal a thousand possibilities beyond Ana. That world was now mine; a world full of beautiful and seductive men and women, interesting and interested in me; so I learnt how to be beautiful again, after all my efforts to forget Ana, to be seductive too, with that special charm of the man-well-on-the-way-to-maturity-who-has-been-marked-by-a-great-love-affair-that-ended, although I'm discreet enough never to touch on the subject. The truth is that I've never told anyone about Ana. No one has ever found out her. I've never shared her with anyone, and nobody has ever found out about what happened when and after Ana left me.

Maybe, now that so much time has past, it's because of all these things that, when I get home from work in the evenings around eight at night, through the living room window I can still see some traces of gold and red behind the buildings in Pinheiros. As I pick up the countless messages, invitations and offers on the answering machine, I still have the strange sensation, even though everything has changed and I'm fine now, that this day is still the same one, like a clock which has stopped, stuck at the same moment – that moment. As if when Ana left me there was no sequel and I just went on standing here until today in the middle of the living-room which used to be ours, with her last note in my hands. My tie loosened slightly at the neck; it was and is so hot that I can feel the sweat running over my body, trickling down my chest, down my arms, to my wrists and then over the palms of my hands which are holding Ana's last note, dissolving the ink from which she had composed the words that are now gradually being erased, washed away by sweat, but which I can't forget, however much time passes and however much, somehow and without Ana, I manage to carry on. Words that say hard, dry, simple, irrevocable things. That Ana has left me, that she's never coming back, that it's pointless trying to find her and, finally, that however hard I fight it, it's forever. And, forever, now, I feel like an opaque soap bubble, suspended in the middle of the living-room, waiting for a chance gust of wind from the open window to carry it off, or for someone to prick that stupid bubble with a pin and make it burst suddenly in the bluish air that looks more like something inside a fish tank, and disappear without leaving a trace.

V

Missing Audrey Hepburn

'like Billie Holiday I'm alone in the desolate dark'
(Ricardo Redisch: *If You Thrash About You'll Drown*)

He lost him as soon as he'd found him, one Saint John's Eve. He didn't know he was going to lose him, he didn't even know that he'd find him. He didn't even know what night it was – it was June, Saint John's Eve. But that was how it happened. He wasn't in the least bit drunk, and he hadn't smoked or sniffed anything. Perhaps all that self-denial was the reason for him finishing up like that, completely lost and mixed up with those types: the Blonde Panther Ready to do Anything for a Higher Status, the Lesbian Who Had Come Out and the Rather Sordid Patriarch Escaped from the Pages of Satyricon. Lost, they'd all managed to lose themselves. He'd lost himself along the viaducts of São Paolo with a book in his hands, struggling not to drown, unsure as to whether he should go back or carry on, for there were fires burning that night, although he didn't know that then. Consulting the almanac later, he'd find out that the waning moon had been in Pisces – which would go some way to explain the spiritual illusions, the false omens, the mists. Mirages, Neptune.

It was Wednesday, he was wearing the God Shango's red and white amulet. The same amulet that some time afterwards would unexpectedly snap and break into pieces as he took off the last item of clothing before going to bed with someone or other. The incident didn't inspire fear of death because this quasi-story belongs to a time when love wasn't a fatal disease. Naked, propped up on one elbow, the Someone Or Other quoted Marx, talked about spiritualism and waited, not really understanding, until the scattered red and white beads had been gathered up, one by one, from the floor. He put them on the table and as he did so he told himself that one day he'd throw them into the sea or into running water. They were in the middle of the countryside, the fire, which had crackled like a fire in an English novel, had died down and now they had to warm their bodies with tongues and fingers in the pretence that they were quenching their thirst, their cold and their lust for betrayal.

His index finger, the nail stained with typewriter ink, searches through the thirty days of the month of June in the *Thinker's Almanac*: Saturday 20th – Ciríaco, Florentina; Sunday 21st – Luis Gonzaga, Márcia; Monday 22nd - Tomás, Joana; Tuesday 23rd – José, Agripina; Wednesday 24th - John the Baptist, Faustino. On the viaduct, he remembered the attack, a year before, a flick-knife – click, your money, mate. Perhaps that's why he breaks off now to go to the bathroom, where he looks at his face in the mirror without seeing anything specific, except two deepening lines at the corners of his mouth, the marks of the god Ogoun, then he slowly washes his hands with flower-scented soap, rubs on some lavender water, breathes; waiting for the phone to ring and save him at least momentarily, from this moment he can't decipher or describe. The phone doesn't ring and – no promises, no pledges – he carries on remembering. So dangerous, even though it's in the past.

A radiant aura, he'd be lying now if he said something like: the temptation was strong, there was a kind of radiant aura over the viaduct where he was wandering around lost, unable to choose a direction. For viaducts, you know, only lead one way, whether you want to go there or not. For a while now he couldn't remember any auras or lights. All he really remembers is that he went back in search of a café, a bar, a cigarette, maybe a brandy to help him understand what was happening. But nothing was happening. The only thing for it was to take a taxi, give the address, with a book in his hands, remark on the weather, the crisis, sneak a look at the tarts, whores and transvestites on the street corners, feel raunchy, pass straight down the avenue and the neon signs for Coca-Cola, Melita and Galaxy, turn left, turn right, straight ahead; complain, pay, get out.

(Later the same evening, before going to bed, he would make a note, perhaps mistaken, and totally obvious; *life is dynamic.*)

It was then he saw the fire for Saint John's Eve. Next to the fire, two boys were lighting a huge red and white hot air balloon. In Shango's colours, because Shango is Saint John. By the popcorn stand the hurdy-gurdy man was cranking out a tune. But there was no parrot or monkey with a cup in its hand and no parakeet doing the lucky dip – you-will-meet-your-love-on-a-Sunday-afternoon-in-the-sign-of-Libra. He must have blinked, for as well as being dynamic, folkloric and slightly frenetic, life seemed to him at that moment too vivid, so many people bustling about and saying things like how nice you've turned up the stars are looking good have something to drink darling. He kissed the Psychoanalyst At Odds With the Elitism Of Her Own Profession, but only shook hands with the Postgraduate Student Uncertain Whether To Admit To His Evident Homosexuality, and left it at that, exchanged a couple of quite amiable words with the Writer Who Was More Successful In Italy Than In Brazil. Then he hung about, accepting everything that came around on the lavish trays: pine nuts, hot toddies, corn porridge, maize cakes baked in banana leaves. Everything you could possibly want at a June festival was there.

Now he slowly empties the ashtray into the Amerindian

wastepaper basket, while gazing at the expression on the face of the woman sitting in front of the glass of absinthe in the cheap Degas print. He thinks that he's thinking or that he should be thinking or it's as if he were thinking something along the lines of that's how people behave when they can't discern a promise or an invitation in the other person's eyes. Or rather, since nothing in his eyes or gesture or vibratory field betrayed that he was looking for someone to share his bed in the coming hours of the cool and therefore favourable night for such adventures, he was automatically left in peace. Or worse still, to one side. Left to one side, next to the fire, with a book he would read later, Redisch's *If You Thrash About You'll Drown*, to find lines like: *a conversation that warms you to your bones without exactly saying anything*. Now he was little more than a camera recording silently and impersonally all those June-ish urban excesses.

Flashback:

They would write names on moistened scraps of paper, which they stuck on the rim of the enamel basin. Then a paper boat would slowly float across and stop at one of the names: Naira, Roselene, Juçara, Ilone, Dulcinha, Valéria, Marília, Vera. Did he already know, back then? One of Paulo Antonio's eyebrows stuck out across his forehead towards his hair. Nelson, all freckles and pert bum, chattered on in his shrill voice. Twenty-one drops dripped from a lighted candle into the water in the basin, until they formed a letter, an initial; M for Marcos or Maria; C for Clara or Celso; R for Ricardo or Regina. He'd have to hop over the fire, if he stepped on the embers he'd wet the bed. At the stroke of midnight, with a lighted candle in his hand, he'd look down into the well, to see the future. Corpse in a coffin – certain death. Wedding-dress – marriage coming. A rose – young love. At midnight he had a look. Nothing. Just the dark bottom of the well, stray reflections, stars, fires, toads hopping, crah-ah-ah-ah-ah, concentric rings, the smell of slime. That was what it was like, the future. Afterwards roads, flags, arrests, exiles, beatings, viaducts, locked doors, revelations, couches, swamps, rainbows. So many, many things – and no one. The ray bore seven fry, each sharply barbed and ready to cling fast to her the moment when the hook pulled her from the bed of the river Uruguay and she was flung into the bottom of the punt. Staining the rags in shades of orange, then pinning it to the eight bright staves, with little tacks and yellow line. From the pinball arcade next to Jeca's place to the corner of Republic Square there were a thousand possibilities, all furtive. And maybe now they're fatal. I will throw the coins of the I Ching six times to find Fire over Fire, The Clinging. Everything will confirm it. But nothing will happen. Oh it's familiar, that everlasting 'will'. And after that, years went by. The years when they were lost to each other, and never again did they find each other.

He clutched the book between fingers turned suddenly cold, then put it on his lap in order to be able to kneel and stretch his hands towards the fire. Me, standing at the door at four in the morning. You, going away. Me, losing myself, becoming helpless amongst the full ashtrays and empty bottles. You, going away. Me, unsure whether to have a bit more to drink or search, completely wasted, for a roach to smoke or glasses to wash; should I plump up the sofas, or put the records away; should I chew over a line from a poem to sweeten the inevitable, bitter awakening and then go to bed, leave, die, sleep, dream maybe. You, going away. Waking up the next morning with the taste of bannister rails in my mouth, the frustration rather than the hangover; a generalised disgust which no aspirin will cure. Would the phone ring? You, going away, a repeat frame. Editing it in. You, going away, you, going away.

It crackled, the firewood crackled like a fire in an English novel. A bright aura. Surrounding the fire, maybe inside it, were adrenalin stained memories, driven out by too much coffee, too many Augusts. As he wouldn't try suicide for the fifth time, not, he counted, even the fifth suc-ces-sive time, (he had been spared that after so many years of analysis) and since permanent crisis seemed the most stable way of surviving, and no one had thought of murdering him or asking him to marry them, and because he could look around and in less than a minute choose someone to chat to, saying things such as, I haven't seen you around lately, and well then, go on, what else have you got to tell me, have another – in the name of all that, he went on, but without much conviction.

Oh Saint John, boy-child Shango/in the fire of Saint John/I always want to be the boy-child, Shango/in the fire and in my mind – he silently hummed in silence the words from a song by Veloso and Gil. As the red and white balloon began its ascent there was no sign of drizzle. Everyone applauded, illuminated by the flames of the fire, they all looked like madmen weary of their own madness. He applauded too, Asshay! It was then that the girl next to him said that she had to go, there were two Audrey Hepburn films on the TV. (*Flashback*: Nara Claudina would say *Puber*, Carlos Renato would correct her: *Hhhe-p-burrn*. One green, green Aquarius afternoon, how many years before he hanged himself in the bathroom? Must have been a lot of years, obviously, because in those days, that afternoon, even the dresses, as well as being pleated, had bobbles and loops.) A sharp jawline, Audrey, huge eyes, always staring, a long-necked gazelle with slender, elongated feet, delicately shod in Chanel shoes, and a suit, always a light beige or sea green suit, hands with infinitely long fingers and unvarnished nails. Anastasia, the forgotten princess. At the matinées in the Imperial cinema.

Belgian, he said, I'm sure. She was Belgian. Belgium, capital Brussels, where we were arrested – and it was so crazy now, something reminding him of something else, more so as time passed – because of our long hair, our brightly-coloured clothes; a city of grey suits and black patent-leather shoes with pointed toes. It's all a long time ago. Now you send me postcards from deepest Norway while I take on everyday tropical demons with coarse salt, amulets, charms, incense-sticks, rosemary, rue, basil, roses of Oshun: now then yeh-yeh-ho! I'm certain it wasn't there but in Holland, that we walked through fields of tulips that shone so brightly they looked artificial. And – Good God! – maybe they were. There was a bridge, then a late train and an August sun above our heads. There'd be no room for Audrey there, with all those towers, squares and bridges, I can see that. But why torture yourself so much? Every morning you unconsciously turn off the alarm clock to stop it jerking you abruptly into the middle of another empty day. Yet more time to be filled only with what you manage to invent. Why not take some evening course or other in the winter? *Alchemic Mandalas and the Architecture of Gothic Cathedrals* for example, or *Sanskrit Prefixes in the Work of Guimarães Rosa* , or even *Post-Modern Premonitions in the Cinema of J.B. Tanko*. Oh, going down Augusta Street at seventy-five miles an hour, high boots, wearing gypsy earrings on the deck of the caravel, a black leather jacket, early mornings, blasts from the open exhausts of motorbikes. No one will hear the dry sound your heels make striking the concrete of dirty pavements. And it's not even Gervaise, Flower of Degradation, coarse and beautiful...

As the girl rose to leave he finally summoned up his courage, drank another swig of toddy and asked, 'Do you know what really happened when the Queen of Transylvania gently took Audrey's chin in a hand covered with rings and said, '*Charming, so charming*'? The girl modestly lowered her eyes. 'That was exactly what Audrey did', he explained.

And he left before her, *no sex, baby*. The hot air balloon was slowly burning where it had landed on the corner. Tomorrow, two months ago or twelve, depending on your point of view, he checked; exactly twenty-five, a Thursday, the day of Oshossi, Guilherme and Lucia.

But only much later, like a strange premonitory flash-back, in the middle of a night of mysterious possession, as he looked in vain for a piece by Charlie Parker, wandering around the house crammed full of good luck charms that didn't work, would he piece back together step by step that Saint John's Eve when he had been allowed to have him, totally, between a sad blues and an avant-garde poem. Or a bright up-tempo blues and an old sonnet. In any case, he could have loved him so much. And loving so much, when it's allowed, should alter one's life. He saw that. For him it was his deepest conviction; almost an ideology or a geography, slowly advancing deeper and deeper with every millimetre into someone else's body, and raising a flag on the conquered territory. Akin to when, looking down, the goddess takes pity and pours a fleeting drop of nectar from her amphora onto our heads. Even if afterwards comes a time of salt, not a time of honey.

There were no amphorae, there was no nectar. An even crueller, but temporary disillusionment, in the time of salt: no goddesses. But after plunging the tip of the diamond needle deep into the black surface, unleashing the Long Moaning Sax Solo, after all, he could still go to the kitchen and make something like a modest mapuche tea, repeating repeating repeating like a scratched record, so distracted that he couldn't weep even a single tear in the night – and such a pretty night too – when they met and lost each other for ever, repeating, and no one would understand, I warned you, repeating in a sigh soaked with memories which no one can put right: oh how much, but how much, how very, very much I miss that thin girl called Audrey Hepburn.

VI

The Saddest Boy in the World

'They're the ones who come from nowhere and leave for nowhere. Someone who suddenly appears, and no one knows where he's come from or where he's going. *Un homme de nulle part.*'

(Nelson Brissac Peixoto: *Stage Sets in Ruins*)

In an aquarium of dirty water, they swim through night and night fog but don't see me; they're fish, blind, ignorant of their inexorable path towards each other and me. In the middle of freezing winter, August, early morning on the corner by the funeral parlour, they swim about amongst punks, beggars, neon lights, prostitutes and moaning synthesizers – sounds, algae, water – floating free in the space which separates the scabrous bar from the darkness of the park, in the town which does not and will not belong to either of them again. For towns, like casual acquaintances and rented apartments, were made to be abandoned – he reflects on this as he swims about.

Him: this man, almost forty, starting to drink just a bit too much, not a lot, just enough to rekindle tired emotions, and thinning out on top, not a lot, but enough to attract a few pathetic jibes. Drops of dew, crystals of fog fall onto that hair-free zone on the top of his head, and beneath it collect certain late night thoughts, a bit of alcohol and a great deal of solitude. He lights a damp cigarette, turns the collar of his grey raincoat up to his ears. In that gesture, the hand holding the cigarette brushes against the roughness of his three-day-old beard. Then he sighs, freezing.

There are a lot of other things one could say about this man on that foggy night, in this bar which I go into now, in this town which was once his town. But standing here, at the back of the same bar which he is entering, without a past, for men of almost forty who walk about alone in the early hours have no past – all these rather vague, rather stupid things, are all I can say about him. Thin, wet, slightly bent over with his thinness, with the cold and with unease. The unease typical of men of nearly forty wandering the nights in towns that, because they have ceased to be their own, have become even less familiar than any other towns.

The bar is just like a long *Danzig Corridor*. The walls are bounded – on the right as you enter, but on the left from where I'm watching – by the long counter and, on the opposite side, by the single row of cheap tables with imitation marble tops. He moves – thin, bent and wet – amongst the tangled web of people along the line, which extends horizontally from the front door to the jukebox at the back where I'm standing and watching. Sombre clothes, a black hulk, a monster spewed up by the nocturnal waves onto the dirty sand of the bar. Amongst these people, although dressed in grey, he seems all white.

The man asks for a beer at the counter, then disappears again amidst the people. Craning my neck, I can only just make out the top of his balding head, until he spots the empty chair at the table where that boy is sitting. And from where I'm standing, beside the jukebox near the corridor which disappears into the dim light of the filthy toilets, I can see them and hear them perfectly well through the whiff of beer, toilet freshener and piss which assails our nostrils.

From the jukebox, to feed this meeting which they haven't realised they're having yet, to help them swim about better in this thing which is still nameless and which they wouldn't even be able to see, if I didn't help them, I will choose: slow blues, soulful sax solos, slow trickling piano on the verge of ecstasy, breathy clarinets and deep voices, dark hoarse voices rough from cigarettes, but velvety from sipping bourbon or brandy. Now everything flows like a golden draught from other waters, not these, that are so cloudy, from which two poor fish have emerged blind from the night, eternally ignorant of my presence next to the jukebox, beside the corridor which leads to the filthy toilets; here, creating impossible lucidities and crooning baleful lullabies for them in their unexpected meeting – a meeting unexpected both by them, as they swim blindly about, and by me, a rodless fisherman looking down over the water which separates us.

Him, there, the one I'm gazing at now, the boy sitting opposite the empty chair in which the man in the grey raincoat sits down, carrying his beer. A boy of almost twenty, drinking a bit too much, not a lot – like boys of almost twenty tend to do when they don't yet know the limits and dangers of the game – with a few pimples, not many, the traces of adolescence scattered across his white face, amongst sparse wisps of the beard which hasn't yet found that precise, definitive shape sketched out on the faces of men of nearly forty, such as the man who's sitting opposite him. Behind the pimples, amongst the wisps of shapeless beard, certain thoughts are collecting – thickened by fog, a little alcohol and a great deal of solitude. The boy over there lights a damp cigarette, turns down the collar of his black jacket, and brushes from his frayed lapel some ash, strands of hair, dust, drops of water. Then he sighs, freezing. He looks around as if he hasn't seen anything or anyone. Not even that man sitting opposite him, who apparently doesn't see him either.

There are a lot of other things one could say about that boy on this gloomy night, in this town where he's always belonged, in this bar where he now sits opposite a man who is a complete stranger to him. But standing here at the back of the same bar in which he sits, contemplating his dismal little past and his lack of a future – for the future of boys under twenty is always obscure, almost invisible – these vague banalities are all I have to offer. He's slight, wet and a little stooped with thinness and the cold; with that unease typical of boys who have not yet learnt the dangers or the pleasures of the game. If that's what it is, a game.

If only I were great Zeus Olympus I'd destroy the city with flaming thunderbolts just to live the moment of the thunderbolt's electric glare. That's what the boy over there would say, with the predictable arrogance of youth. Not now though, for the moment he doesn't say anything. Neither he nor the man of almost forty speaks. They sit opposite each other at the table to the left of where I'm standing, next to the jukebox, to the right as you enter; strategically placed to watch those who have emerged from the night and the fog in which they were floundering blindly outside; before they came into this bar. Before I sucked them in with my eyes, greedy for other people's encounters, giving them life, even this precarious, paper life, where Greek Zeus and Brazilian Oshalá Tupan also exercise their power over their predestined simulacra.

No, they don't say anything. There is enough noise around to spare them the need for words, which might be, who can say, harsh ones. Or maybe, on the contrary, they might provide an unbearable balm for the burning throats of those who prowl the nights as they do, as I do, as we do. Their words can be put off. Mine cannot.

For the time being, they look about them. They deliberately don't look each other in the face; even though they are both thin and stooping slightly as a result; even though both are damp from the fog outside; even though one is dressed in grey and the other in black (as the times demand if one is not to be rejected); even though both are drinking rather warm beer (although it doesn't matter much what you drink in this bar provided you drink) and though they are smoking similarly crumpled cigarettes – sad, poor quality cigarettes of the kind that only solitary, nocturnal men rummage through coat pockets for in the early hours of the morning, whether they are twenty or forty years old. Or older, or younger – solitary men are ageless. Even though they are freezing, giddy from alcohol, stiff with cold, lucid from that solitude which pursues like a fury those men without a past or a future, a wife or a friend, family or property. They don't look at each other.

They are unaware of each other. For they sense that – I am inventing this; Lord over my absurd inventions, because I too am living them, as I create – if they yield to each other's solitude, there will be no space left for escape: no drunken screw with someone whose face you won't remember two days later; no snort of coke on the street corner; no sordid piss next to the waiter who has no hang-ups, but is understanding about whatever anyone else does for their kicks; no hasty joint in the mud of the park. Things like that, you know? I do: loving what is oneself in someone else can sometimes chain you down, but when bodies touch one another minds can fly much further than the horizon.

So they don't look at each other. And it's not me who decides that, it's them. One shouldn't look, not when looking would mean peering into a mirror which might be cracked, distorting – injurious. So I hesitate, do I spend my token on Bessie Smith or Louis Armstrong (everything is imaginary tonight in this bar, including the jukebox which is actually full of other more fashionable ways to ease the time), to better smooth the flow, unjam the traffic, make things sweeter or more bitter? Fearing though that boys under twenty won't yet be able to appreciate such crowded abysses, the dark, nocturnal exquisiteness of husky voices against a background of blue velvet plush in some place other than this Danzig Corridor in a provincial town whose name I've forgotten, we've forgotten. Sophistication, posing; weariness and arm length gloves.

Mine, theirs. For there are three of us and one. The one who is watching from outside, the one who is watching from afar, the one who has been watching since very early on. This one, foreseeing it all. Those three, surprised, shocked. Watching from within, entangled. Four of us now?

For then it begins. But it begins in such a banal way – what's your name, what's your sign, would you like another beer, can I have a cigarette, I haven't got any money on me, I'll pay, it's all right, what are you doing around here, seeing what turns up, do you always come here, it's so cold – that I almost hit the button for some new sounds, replace the husky tones that I'm imagining with the tense cry of an electric bass enabling them to revel in the shrillness of the night. But suddenly they both come to terms with each other – this man in the grey raincoat, that boy in the black jacket, together at the same table – and without having to be prepared for it, although I was, for I was the one who set this trap, suddenly they look directly and deeply into each other's eyes. Beside the dark hulk, the sea monster, in the midst of the smell of beer and piss, amongst the white tiles on the walls of the bar, like a huge toilet buried in the middle of the night in which they are lost – they find each other and look at each other.

They acknowledge each other, finally they agree to acknowledge each other. They light each other's crumpled cigarettes with sureness and a certain, still timid, tenderness. They discreetly share a beer. They watch each other with a certain aloofness, precision, method, order, discipline. Without either surprise or desire, for that boy with the black jacket, uneven beard and a few pimples couldn't be the man who that man with the bald patch on the top of his head would desire, if he desired other men, and perhaps he does. And vice-versa: that boy, even if he were maybe someone capable of such impetuosity, wouldn't want that man in the palm of his hand, thinking up crazy ideas in the silence of his bedroom, which is doubtless full of pennants, superheroes, stickers and all the vestiges of a time barely over, when it was too early to know whether one has an unavoidable desire for someone of one's own kind. Maybe he does. But this man, that boy – no. It doesn't happen like that.

They watch each other without desire. They watch each other mildly, disarmed, with complicity, abandonment, poignantly, sternly, like comrades. Moved to pity. They assemble words that reach me in broken fragments across the distance which separates us, in the form of gentle, hesitant questions which veil in caution and enchantment a recognition which has ceased to be nocturnal and that has become something else which I have not yet named, and I don't know whether I shall, so bright that it threatens to blind me too. I hold back the word, as they now see something that is just revealing its shape, and to me it is beautiful.

The boy looks at his arms and says, see how thin I am? When I hold a chick in my arms – that's just what he says, chick, and the man blinks slightly, discreetly, so as not to emphasise the twenty-year gulf between them – I look at my arms, too feeble to hold a woman tight, and then I start to fantasize about muscles I haven't got, because I'm so weak, because I'm so thin, because I'm so young. The boy looks coolly around him, without even a glimmer of passion in his pale white face, and adds, I want to kill myself, I can't see any point in living, I haven't got a father, every day my mother shakes me and shouts wake up, get up you layabout, go to work. I want to read poetry, I've never had a friend, I've never had a letter sent to me. I walk around the bars at night, I'm afraid to sleep, I'm afraid to wake up, I end up playing snooker into the small hours of the morning and going to bed when the sun's coming up and I've got completely drunk. I was born at a time when everything came to an end, I haven't got any future, I don't believe in anything – he doesn't say that, but I hear it, and so does the man opposite him, and so does the whole bar. Then the man answers, with that kind of sober wisdom which men of almost forty inevitably acquire.

He, the man, runs the palm of his hand through his thin hair, as if he were caressing the time that has past, and he says, the man says, don't be afraid, it'll pass. Don't be afraid, kid. You'll find a right way, even if the right way doesn't exist. But you'll find your way, and that's what matters. If you can hold on, it might even be good. The man gets his wallet out of his pocket, orders another beer and a fresh packet of cigarettes, then he looks with moist eyes at the boy and this is what he says. No, he doesn't actually say anything. He looks at the boy with moist eyes. For a long time, a man of almost forty looks with moist eyes at a boy of almost twenty, whom he has never seen before, in the middle of a bar in the middle of this town which isn't his any more. While he looks, and he takes a long look, the man discovers what I too discover at that same moment.

That boy with the black jacket, a few pimples, an uneven beard and skin that's too white – that boy is the saddest boy in the world.

And to make all these things even more absurd, or at least improbable, the tomorrow which is already today will be Fathers' Day. Bewildered by dates which mean nothing to those who have nothing, the man of almost forty, who does not have sons to strengthen the solitary part of him, begins to explain how he's come from another town to see his father. He speaks in the same desolate tone as the boy who now and forever has become the saddest boy in the world, exactly as he used to be, but never will be again, yet will never cease to be, and says, they don't look at me, they sit there in that family security they've built up which won't allow anything or anyone that might disturb their false peace, and they don't look at me, they don't see me, they don't know what I am. They water me down, they make me invisible, they limit me to the unbearable limits of what they have chosen to tolerate, and which I can't tolerate – do you understand?

The boy less than twenty hardly understands. But he stretches his hand across the table and touches the hand of the man who is nearly forty. Their fingers join together. There is so much thirst between them, between us.

Much time has passed. Dawn is about to break. It's colder. The bar is half empty, it's nearly time to shut. Slumped over the till, the owner is asleep. I've spent nearly all my jukebox tokens – it's all blues, blue and gentle pain. I've got just one left, which I'm definitely going to risk on Tom Waits. I get ready. Then – as the waiters pile chairs on top of the empty tables, a little annoyed with me, the one who is inventing and nourishing all of this, and with these two strange guys, they look like two queers holding hands, crazy, madly in love with someone who is not the other, but could be, if they were that daring and didn't have to leave – the man tightens his grip on the two hands of the saddest boy in the world. Their four hands squeeze each other, warm each other, mingle with each other, comfort each other. Not a black, slimy sea monster, spewed up in the morning. But a white starfish. A five pointed star, mother-of-pearl. A half-opened oyster displaying the black pearl torn from the night and from sickness, pure blues. And he says, the man says,

'You don't really exist. I don't really exist. But my thirst is so powerful that I have invented you to quench it and you are so strong in your fragility that you have invented me to quench your own thirst. We have invented each other because we were all we needed to carry on living. And because we invented each other, I am granting you power over my destiny and you are granting me power over your destiny. You are giving me your future, I am offering you my past. And so like this we are present, past and future. Infinite time all in one, eternity.'

In this bar with the chairs stacked up, the only table left is the one where the two of them remain sitting, oblivious to the debris of that stage set. From my corner, I watch. There is bound to be some tart slumped in a corner, some little faggot jerking a black man off in the toilet. I don't see them. For the time being I don't. From my corner, I can only see these different, identical men, their four hands clasped on the cheap, imitation marble table top.

And it's then that the boy says how he's been delivering flowers all day, that he's got some money together, he's struggled to save a hundred bucks, some petty little amount like that, stuff that would mean something to boys less than twenty, and he insists, magnificently, on paying for the last beer. Everything is the last, now. There are no other bars open in the town. A vitreous light begins to break through the night fog in which we're all still plunged, you included; myopic fish screwing up our eyes to see each other close up, and we do. Beautiful, frightening; our gills quiver. The man takes his wallet out again, full of notes and cheques and credit cards, one of those bulging wallets that only men of nearly forty manage to acquire, but which mean nothing at moments like this. The boy insists, the man gives in, and puts away his wallet. The last waiter brings the last beer. I put my last token in the jukebox, for the last blues. No one sees, no one hears anything else as the approach of morning lulls all crazy thoughts to sleep. Will you remember, tomorrow?

Tender, pale, real; they look at each other. They caress each other's hands, then arms, shoulders, necks, faces, the features on their faces, their hair. With that sweetness born between two men alone in the middle of a freezing night, a little drunk and there's nothing for it but to love each other like this, more passionately than they would love each other if they were hunting for another body, the same as or different from their own – what does it matter, there is nothing but thirst. From where I am, I can see the souls of these two shining. Pale yellow, bright violet; dancing over the rubbish.

They weep as they caress each other. A man of almost forty and a boy less than twenty, ageless both of them.

I am both of them, I am the three of us, I am the four of us. Those two who are meeting, this third one who is watching and telling, this fourth one who is listening. We are one – this one who looks without finding and, when he does find someone, usually can't bear the actual meeting which denies the destiny he had always seen as his own. The one he is seeking must not exist, otherwise the itinerary will have to be replanned to introduce *Tui*, The Joyous. And happiness is The Lake, not the cloudy aquarium, fog and hazy words; Neptune, astral conjunctions. And perhaps he does exist, at least to quench his thirst for the time that has passed, for the time that has not come, for the time that one imagines, invents or counts on. In short, for time.

This strange, semi-divine power leaves me even more dizzy than they are, as they get up and lingeringly embrace at the door of the bar, after paying the bill. Lovers, relatives, equals: strangers.

Then the boy goes, for he has other paths to tread. The man stays, for he too has his path. He follows the shadow of the departing boy with exactly the same gaze as that with which I follow the shadow of the man standing for a moment at the door of the bar, but he won't stay; this is no longer his town. The boy will remain; because it's in this town that he must choose (if one ever really chooses anything): a path, a destiny, a story – his vague future – then, when it's over, he must kill it (if one ever really kills anything). Tom Waits' hoarse voice repeats over and over that this is the time, and that there will be time, just like in a poem by T.S.Eliot, and yes, it must be true – even as the last waiter gently touches the shoulder of the man in the grey raincoat, his hair thinning on top, almost forty, standing at the door of the bar. Discreetly, amicably, pointing at the figure of the saddest boy in the world as he goes off to catch the first bus, the waiter asks:

'Is he your son?'

From where I'm standing, beside the now silent jukebox, I catch an inexplicable scent of fresh roses; as if dawn had come and spring suddenly erupted in the park opposite – I've got nothing against happy endings. Before the man goes, I see him smile kindly and then, lying to the waiter, he says yes, no, who knows. And whatever he says, like whatever I say, will be true. From here, where I am left standing, I know that there are still three and four of us. I their father, I their son, I themselves, plus you; the four of us, a single man lost in the night, sunk in this aquarium of dirty water that reflects the neon lights. A blind fish ignorant of my inevitable path towards the other whom I contemplate with moist eyes from afar, without the courage to touch him. In the middle of the night: a certain craziness, a little alcohol and a great solitude.

I'd like another whisky, another career. Everything is gradually turning to day, and life..., life can be fear and honey when you abandon yourself and look, even from afar.

No, I don't want or need anything if you touch me. I stretch out my hand.

Then I sigh, freezing. And I leave you.

VII

The Little Red Shoes

'– You shall dance – said the angel. – You shall dance in your red shoes... You shall dance from door to door... You shall dance, you shall dance for ever.'

(Hans Christian Andersen: *The Little Red Shoes*)

1

So it was over. Because you know, something inside you always knows exactly when it's about to end – she repeated in front of the mirror, looking herself straight in the eyes. Or when it's just beginning: a certain leap in the pit of your stomach. Like the car on the Big Dipper, when you're right at the top, just before you plunge towards...towards what? After so many ups and downs, towards that unbearable barren point which is now.

There was nothing for it but to light another cigarette, and that's what she did. As she took the first drag, she rested her face in her hands and, without thinking, stretched taut the skin below her right eye. That was better, much better. Get rid of that shattered look, the weariness you can't hide of a lonely woman who's nearly forty. She chewed continuously, relentlessly. With the fingers of her left hand she pulled down the skin below her other eye too. No, not too much, that made her look Japanese. A Jap, a geisha, that was it. The submissive little whore choreographing candle-lit dinners – Glenn Miller or Charles Aznavour? Mischievously pouring in the bath salts – camomile or lavender? Fixing him his Scotch – one or two ice cubes today, darling?

None, she decided. And she tipped the bottle once more into the glass. She had learnt that from him, she never used to like it. A waste of time, a sheer waste of time. And don't you tell me: but it had its good moments, didn't it? His head abandoned on her lap, and you slowly running your fingers through that man's hair. If you could only see your own face at moments like that you'd begin to shine and smile invisibly, with your eyes closed, blooming. Didn't that make it all worthwhile, Adelina?

She took another sip, a little hastily. She had to hurry, before Thursday turned into Good Friday and her memory started teeming with sins like monkeys in a cage: don't drink, don't sing, don't swear, don't wear red, the devil's loose, he'll carry your soul off to hell. She's there now, in the midst of the flames, poor lost soul, not even ten in the evening, just religious films on the TV, holy vestments, that sort of thing, Good Friday and no sex, not even any sex, all that sticking it in, biting, moaning, coming, sleeping. All that smooth stuff, that bare skin stuff, that stuff under the sheets, that stuff in the dark, the moist rubbing together of hair, saliva and sighs after...just how long was it? Five, five years. Five years are really something when you're nearly forty, and no apartment of your own, no husband, children or inheritance; nothing. A barren point, a dead point.

Hey, wasn't that your *choice*? He stood there then in front of her, very dignified, quite the well-behaved head-of-the-family-from-Vila-Mariana in his smooth grey suit, his tie a little lighter, just the same shade as his socks, and slightly darker shoes. Totally in control, not a hair out of place as he repeated deliberately, didactically, convincingly, but Adelina, you know as well as I do, maybe even better, how much our relationship's deteriorated. He must speak just like that to his students, you can't possibly fail to see how painful it is for me to face our breaking up like this. After all, the affection I cherish for you is real.

Did he actually go so far as to say *cherish*? Yes, he must have done, he must have said cherish & relationship & breaking up & affection, he must have said respect, too, & consideration & highest regard and all that polite crap that people usually say to liven up their indifference when their heart has turned completely frigid. A stalactite...stalactite or stalagmite? Shit, one hangs down, the other goes up, but what does it matter; a spindly shaft of sharpened ice thrust with the utmost cordiality deep into her breast. Like a vampire, she would slowly age hundreds and hundreds of years until she crumbled into dust at his impassive feet. But it wasn't like that at all, she sat there so forlorn, barefoot, almost naked, without any make-up or a guardian angel, in an old brush-nylon nightie, the night before Good Friday, alone in the apartment and on the planet Earth.

She stubbed out her cigarette and lowered her head as if she were going to cry. But she bravely decided she wouldn't weep a single tear and gazed down at her bare feet. Little feet, almost like a child's, with unvarnished nails, buried in the yellow rug in front of the dressing table. It was then she remembered the shoes. That Monday, as she tried to put the pieces back together again, she wouldn't be able to say whether she really had needed to light another cigarette or drink another sip of Scotch to help that vague idea take shape. Maybe she had, just before she started flinging open the doors of all the cupboards and chests in search of the shoes. They'd been a present from him when he'd been a bit drunk and more passionate than usual after one of those stupid weekends in Guarujá or Campos do Jordão, such a long time ago. She caught sight of herself in the cheap mirror, slightly distorted from a distance, a woman with dishevelled hair throwing boxes and clothes right and left until she found, in the third drawer of the cupboard, the parcel wrapped in light blue tissue paper.

She carefully unwrapped it. A sudden calm. Almost like a ballerina in her precise, measured, elegant movements. The absolute silence of the empty apartment broken only by the slight rustling of the tissue paper being unfolded quite unhurriedly. And they were lovely, more lovely than she could have remembered. More lovely than she had tried to express when she protested, with restrained emotion, but they're so...so daring, honey, they're not me at all. She who avoided bright colours, heels, make-up, low necklines, gold or any other detail that might be that little bit suggestive of her secret identity as a single-and-independent-woman-with-a-married-lover.

Red, more than just red: crimson, scarlet, blood-red, with thin, extremely high heels and a narrow strap at the ankles. They gleamed in her hands. She almost yielded to the urge to put them on straightaway, but she knew by instinct that she'd have to complete the ritual first. Somehow she had memorised that text so long ago that she just assumed she'd forgotten it. Like a debut postponed for years. The first words, the first movements would be enough for all the stage directions and vocal inflections to be pieced back together again in her memory in the utmost detail. What she would do next would be just perfect, as if it had already been performed and applauded thousands of times.

Perfect. Adelina put on a record, not Charles Aznavour, or Glen Miller, but a lush Billie Holiday number, *I'm glad, you're bad*, taking care to press the button so that the needle would return and keep returning to the beginning, *don't explain*, then she slowly filled the bath with tepid water and sprinkled in some bath salts before sinking in herself, Billie moaning hoarsely in the background, *lover man*, and washed every orifice, her hair too, all her hair, turned to face the cold shower, dried her body and hair while she varnished her fingernails and toenails, in the same shade of red as the shoes, later touching up her mouth with lipstick, having put on the tight black dress, with crepe frills, clipped at the shoulder with a little diamond brooch, flowing down her neck to reveal the top of her breasts, then she highlighted the spot on her right cheek with a pencil, just like Liz Taylor everyone used to say, added some black eyeliner, darkened her lashes, sprinkled perfume in her cleavage, on her wrists, on her throat, behind her ears, so you'll give off such an aroma when you're gasping and panting, my girl, then the see-through black silk stockings, with a seam at the back, a film noir tigress, a Lauren Bacall, and only after putting in her handbag a chequebook, her papers, car keys, cigarettes and the silver lighter which she took out of the little red velvet box, a present on her thirty-seventh birthday, only when she was quite ready from head to toe and had turned off the record player, for they had to have silence, did she sit down again at the dressing table and put on the little red shoes.

  She turned off the bedroom light and looked at herself in the full-length hall mirror. She liked what she saw. She drank the last sip of whisky and, before going out, dropped the white filter stained with lipstick into the golden drop left at the bottom of the glass.

2

There were three of them, and they were together, but the black guy was the first to ask if he could sit down. The only woman on her own in the night club. He had thin features, the black guy, sharp like a white man's, although his lips were fuller, and slightly moist. Muscles bursting out of his close-fitting tee shirt and his tight jeans. The slight smell of a clean animal, a washed animal, but undisguisably an animal beneath the soap:

'So, out for a wander?' he asked, settling himself in the chair opposite her.

She leaned over for him to light her cigarette. His big, square strong black hand stayed where it was on the table. She lit it herself with the silver lighter. Then she threw her head back – the timing was perfect – inhaled deeply and, in the midst of the smoke, uttered these words over the pathetic plastic saucers with peanuts and popcorn:

'You know, it's a bank holiday. The town's empty and all that. You've got to make the most of it, right?'

Under the table, the black guy edged his knee between her thighs. She gave way slightly, at least until she felt the heat rising. But she preferred to cross her legs affectedly. It wasn't going to be as easy as that, just because she was on her own. And nearly in her forties, second-rate flesh, and past it. She smiled at the other one who was leaning at the bar, the golden boy with the looks of a tennis player. Not that he was blonde, but he was that golden colour – like a peach when it's just starting to ripen – all over his skin, his hair too, and probably his eyes which she couldn't see without her glasses from that distance. The black guy followed her gaze, looking round over his shoulder. Sideways on, she noticed, his chin was abrupt, roughly hewn. Although clean shaven, his chin would be scratchy if you ran your hand over it. Before he could say anything, she moved things along, saying very huskily,

'Why don't you invite your friends to sit with us?' He rolled a peanut between his fingers. She took the peanut from his fingers. The crepe slipped off her shoulder to reveal the hollow between her breasts: 'I don't think you'll be needing this.'

The black guy frowned. Then he laughed. He rubbed his forefinger over the back of her hand:

'You'd better believe it.'

She blew the smoke in his face:

'Is that right?'

'I swear.'

She uncrossed her legs. His knee pressed against the inside of her thighs again. I wanna throw you on the floor, the song was saying:

'Call your friends over then.'

'Wouldn't you rather we stayed here on our own, just the two of us?' It was so dark in there that she could hardly see the other one, next to the golden tennis player. A little shorter, maybe. But broad-shouldered. Something in his demeanour, even though he was standing with his back to her, facing the counter, leaning over his drink, something in his firm bottom outlined in the cloth of his trousers – there was something promising about him. She stirred the ice cubes in the Scotch with the tips of her red nails:

'Nice boys. Alone like that. Aren't they your friends?'

'Best buddies', he confirmed. And he pressed his knee harder. Her knickers became damp. 'Good people, both of them.'

'Good people are always welcome', she said as if in a dubbed film. Another woman was moving her body and mouth; she was talking. A black and white, high contrast film, a film she'd never seen, although she knew the story well enough. Because someone had told her, at coffee-time, because she'd seen the posters or had read something in one of those women's magazines she had piled up at home. The most recent ones under the glass-topped living room table. The rest, stacked in the maid's bathroom and mouldy from a continual leak in the shower, would be taken away later by the daily help. To sell, she said. And she felt a pent-up hatred at the thought of the glossy pages of her magazines being used to wrap up fish at the market or displayed on those shabby stalls in the town centre:

'If that's what you really want', said the black guy. And he waited for her to say something, before raising his hand to call the other two over.

'There's nothing I'd like better', she whispered.

And quite suddenly – for after the fourth or fifth Scotch everything always happens like this, and you can't tell exactly when the shift takes place, when one situation becomes another situation, quite suddenly, the golden tennis player was sitting on her right, and the shorter boy on her left. In the chair opposite her, the black guy was watching everything with alert, suspicious eyes. She asked what they were drinking and they said, together and predictably, beer. She said (with a touch of Mae West), for God's sake have something stronger, you're gonna need it boys. The three of them explained in different ways that they were broke, you know, the crisis. The golden tennis player actually turned his pocket inside out and showed her, grabbing her hand, look, take a look, take a hold of it, but she drew her hand away just before she touched it. So close, heat throbbing at her fingertips. No problem, she offered extravagantly, I'll pay. Halfway through the bottle already, she poured some of her Scotch out for the black guy and the golden tennis player. Not for the shorter guy, who preferred vodka, *Natasha* will do fine. It was then that she really looked at him for the first time. Quite small and strong, with very curly hair contrasting with his white skin, red lips, a two or three-day-old beard which almost met the hairs on his chest that were escaping from beneath the collar of his shirt, his hands clasped a little tensely on the chequered tablecloth, his nails bitten down. With his head lowered, concentrated in his smallness, full of the vitality which she could sense, unmistakably, before she had even tasted it.

Patient, excited, enjoying themselves; they fulfilled all the required rituals to get to that point. The black guy's sign was Aries, he was a footballer, next month I'm going into the first division, I'll be earning a packet. Sérgio or Silvio, something like that. The golden tennis player, Ricardo, Roberto, or was it Rogério? a Sagittarian bank clerk, did body building and his chest that he invited her to touch was bulging and rock-hard like a weightlifter's, he dreamed of being a model, I've even had some photos done, if you like one day I'll show you, in the buff, and she thought, he'll end up a rent boy for some rich queen. All she managed to get out of the smaller guy was his sign, Leo, and only then because she guessed it, he didn't reveal his name or say what he did, he was just hanging around, seeing what's what, and he couldn't handle all that socialising bit.

Me? Gil-da, she lied touching up her lipstick. But she was only partly lying, she told her little mirror, because in a kind of way I've always been just Gilda, a Scorpio, and there she was telling the truth, an actress, and now she was lying again, but only in a way, because I've been one all my life.

Then they danced, each of them once. The black guy rested his heavy hand on her waist and, pulling her towards him, locked their groins together almost as if he were penetrating her, to the sound of one of those Roberto Carlos records you hear in motels, concave/convex, so tight and hard that she was afraid she'd wet her knickers. But as they went back to the table and she discreetly felt herself, she put her mind at rest before being pulled out onto the floor again by the golden hand of the golden tennis player. He made her rest her head on his chest, smelling of cologne, deodorant, clean man's sweat beneath the pale yellow polo-neck shirt, licked her ear, nibbled the hollow of her neck to the sound of one of those romantic tracks with words in English from a soap opera, until she moaned, all wet, begging him to stop. The smaller guy didn't want to dance. I want to fuck you, he growled; why all this pussy-footing around?

It was when she lifted her leg, resting her foot on the edge of the chair, that they all saw the red shoe. After their excited comments, the meticulous preparations were all tied up, the club was almost empty, Friday was well and truly here, Passion Friday at that, the raw grey of an urban dawn creeping through the cracks, the single impatient waiter, chairs on the tables. They'd reached that point. The live point, the hot point:

'Where to?' asked the golden tennis player.

'My apartment, where else?' she said as she finished signing the cheque with her imported pen. 'Right then, who do you want to go with?' the black guy wanted to know.

She stroked the smaller guy's face:

'With all three of you of course'.

Despite the whisky she walked steadily out in her red shoes, the three of them following her. Outside, in the morning light, before they got in the car which the parking attendant brought round and the golden tennis player insisted on driving, the red shoes were the only thing that was coloured in that street.

3

Take off everything, except the shoes, they all begged her in the untidy bedroom. A bottle of whisky on the dressing table, an old Fafá de Belém song on the record player (the golden tennis player's choice, the black guy wanted Alcione), an overflowing ashtray on the bedside table. She took everything off, throwing her clothes this way and that. Except the black silk stockings with the seam down the back, and the red shoes. Naked, she flung herself down on the pink chenille bedspread, her legs wide apart. They drew slowly around her, throwing their briefs onto the black crepe.

The black guy took her from behind, that was how he liked it, nice and tight. She'd never done that, but he swore in her ear that he'd be careful, then gave her a bite on her shoulders as he turned her sideways – ever so gently, moistening her with saliva with his finger – so that the shorter guy could carry on licking her between her thighs, while the golden tennis player knelt and rubbed his prick over her face until he found her mouth. It too had a kind of peachy taste, but too green, almost sour, and running her hands down his back she confirmed that earlier suspicion of a soft triangle of down just above his bum, just like the one on his chest, turned a shade of grey by the dawn filtering through the blinds, but golden for sure in the sunlight. It was when the black guy penetrated deeper that she disengaged herself from the golden tennis player and pulled the shorter guy on top of her. He filled her right up, as she had the strange sensation that at some distant point within her, from each side of a purple transparent plastic film, like in a book she'd read, their two members touched each other, head to head. And first she moaned, then thrashed about and tried to find the golden tennis player's golden mouth and almost, almost came. But she preferred to pour another whisky, smoke another cigarette, quite unhurried, for she needed more and they generously gave it, and so it was no surprise at all when they changed places, and the golden tennis player took her from behind just as the smaller guy entered her mouth, and the black guy inside her managed to turn her moans into louder and louder cries, fuck the neighbours, then quieter and quieter again, growling and grunting, until they were just tiny sobs, she'd been through seven galaxies, the star of Vega in the fourteenth degree of Capricorn and her face buried in the black curly hair of his broad black chest. Other ways they tried, every way – four or five times. Standing up in the bathroom, trying to get satisfaction under the cold water of the shower. In the lounge on all fours on the satin cushions, on the sofa, then on the floor. In the kitchen, looking for some liver salts and making coffee, bent over the sink. In front of the full-length hall mirror, not at all shocked when the smaller guy suddenly entered the golden tennis player who was inside her from behind, with her rubbing the black guy's prick until it spurted over her red shoes, with her in the arms of all three of them, and she was no longer Gilda, or Adelina or anything. She was a nameless body, shot through with pleasure, covered in teeth and nail-marks, in the scratches from beard stubble, smeared with the unclaimed milk of the males from the streets. Utterly satisfied. And avenged.

When they finally left, well after midday, before flinging herself on the bed she slowly cleaned the shoes with a face flannel that she then threw in the dirty laundry basket. It was the neon lights, she repeated as she walked around the room, those green, violet and red lights winking opposite the night club, it was the evil neon light of Good Friday, when the devil gets loose because Christ is dead, nailed on the cross. When she turned out the light she just had time to see herself in the dressing table mirror, make-up smeared all over her face, but with an expression of triumph peeping out from amongst her unkempt hair.

She woke up first thing on Easter Saturday, the doorbell piercing her aching head. He was standing there in the corridor, a dozen red roses and an Easter egg in his hands, a smile on his pale lips. She didn't have to say anything. Just smile, too. But she wasn't smiling when she said,

'Go away. It's over.'

Even then he still tried to say something, in that ridiculous grey suit. He actually got part way into the lounge before she pushed him out, shouting, almost completely naked apart from the silk stockings and the extremely high-heeled red shoes. There was a smell of cigarettes and booze and come soaked into every corner of the apartment, the signs of a hangover on her face, the purple marks of love bites on her neck. For the first, only and last time he called her, over and over again, a bitch, a tramp, a perverted, depraved, scummy bitch. He threw the egg and the red roses in her face and went away forever.

Only then did she sit down and take off her shoes. The ankle straps had left deep gashes in the flesh of her swollen ankles. There were cuts all over her toes. She took a very hot bath and tidied the whole house before going back to bed – the diamond brooch had disappeared, but what did it matter, it was imitation – taking two pills to sleep right through the rest of Saturday and Easter Sunday, waking up to eat pieces of the chocolate egg that lay smashed in the lounge.

In the office on Monday, when they saw her walking with difficulty, her hair tied back, dressed in brown, collar buttoned up, and wanted to know what was wrong, new shoes, she explained very simply, too tight, it's nothing. The cuts started to hurt again when it looked like rain. And as she opened the third drawer of the cupboard to see the light blue tissue paper containing the shoes, she felt a slight shudder. She tried – did she really try? – not to give way. But the urge to put them on was almost always strongēr. For after all, she told herself (as if she were in a story by Sonia Coutinho), there are so many Fridays, so many neon lights, so many gorgeous, solitary boys lost in this dirty town. She only thought of throwing them out when her varicose veins started to swell, climbing up her thighs, and then the doctor prodded her groin and later informed her there was something wrong.

VIII

A Little White Sandy Beach, Down by the Gully

'Each man kills the thing he loves.'
(Oscar Wilde, quoted by Fassbinder in *Querelle*).

1

It was exactly seven years ago today that I ran away forever from Passo da Guanxuma, Dudu. It's September, the month of your birthday, but I can't remember which day.

This just came back to me now while I was looking at my face in the mirror trying to decide whether or not to shave. You know what my beard is like, still so stiff and thick. If I shave every day my face gets covered in cuts, ingrowing bristles, red patches. If I don't shave my face starts to look dirty. I couldn't make up my mind. But it was when I looked in the mirror that I saw the calendar next to it and then I got that heavy feeling in my heart, that memory of Passo, of September and you. When I thought of September, I thought of some dumb things too, like little butterflies fluttering about, little flowers breaking through the soil, winds blowing, a sky as blue as if it had been painted by hand. My God, there were so many idiotic things about that town. Still are, right?

Then I looked out of the window. The window in my room looks out onto the back of another building, there's always this grey fug hanging there. A thick, oily fug. If you were here, and you looked straight out you'd see a lot of little bathroom windows but they're too small to get even a glimpse of all the hanky-panky that must be going on behind them. If you looked down you'd see trashcans all piled up in the yard. You'd only see a little patch of sky if you looked up – and when I wrote little patch of sky *I remembered that old tune you liked so much, wasn't it a* chorinho? *I always look up, to see the grey air between my window and the side of the other building stretch up until it merges with the sky; a thick cloak of soot cast over this town that's so far from Passo and everything that's clear, even if it is a bit dumb.*

When I think like that, here in this town Dudu, you've no idea what a crazy, crazy longing I get to go back. But I'm not going back. You know better than absolutely anyone that I can never go back. I just thought about it and was so sure of that I actually started to feel a bit faint and my hand slipped and made that smudge, sorry. I was pressing both my hands against the sheet of paper, as if I wanted to hang on to it. As if there was nothing under my feet.

You don't know this, but that's what happens when you leave a little town that's stopped being yours and go live in another town that hasn't started being yours yet. You always start feeling a bit weird when you think you don't really want to stay but you don't want to – or can't – go back either. You feel just like one of those guys in the circus who walks the tightrope and suddenly the wire breaks, snap! and you're just hanging there, suspended in mid-air, empty space below your feet. With nowhere in the world to go, do you know what I mean?

I'm so alone Dudu. I'm so sad that sometimes I throw myself on the bed, bury my face in the pillow and try to cry. Of course I can't manage it. I let out a few gasps, growls and sobs; animal noises, I grunt like a pig with a knife stuck in its heart. I always think of you at times like that. Today I felt like writing to you instead. The sheets are filthy too. The landlady who rents me this flat only changes them every other week, and it must be getting towards the end of the second week. I've got this thing about buying my meals in the street, in those little tinfoil cartons, I sit there eating on the sheets and before I know it a bit of food's fallen onto them. Rice, omelette, mayonnaise, pizza – that plastic food you eat here – no nice fatty ribs sprinkled with manioc flour, like in Passo.

Apart from all that, which is pretty disgusting, I'm still a nice clean guy Dudu. And if you can still remember those swims we had in the nude in the gully at Caraguatatá – because I haven't forgotten for a single second in all these seven years – you'll know better than anyone how true that is.

2

I'm thirty-three and I'm a really clean guy. I have at least one shower a day, I give my ears a good wipe out with cotton wool buds, the brand with the competition, if you find a gold one you win a prize but I never have. I don't cut my nails, I don't have to, because since I was a kid I've bitten them down to the quick.

I'm not an ugly guy, at least I don't think so. Sure I could be a bit taller but I'm no midget. And I could do with being a bit less hairy. Sometimes I take off all my clothes and look at myself naked in the mirror on the wardrobe door. I've got hair everywhere, when I shave I have to start right where my chest finishes and my neck begins. My chest ends up looking like one of those collarless shirts, a dark tee shirt. If I didn't shave, it would all merge into one. I've got hair on my shoulders too, a bit on my back, then it thins out and only starts again just below my waist, above my bum. Black, curly hair. Where there isn't any hair my skin's very white.

It wasn't like that back in Passo. I don't mean I wasn't hairy, that started when I was thirteen or fourteen, and it hasn't stopped since. Hair is the kind of thing that never stops growing on a guy's body. But my skin, that's what I mean, my skin didn't used to be white. In Passo it was sunny almost every day, and there was the little white sandy beach down by the gully. I'd lie there on the sand, stark naked, almost always alone. I'd swim and swim and swim in that clean water. That must be why, underneath all this hair, my muscles are so firm.

Or they used to be. I've spent such a long time lying down that they're getting flabby. That's just one of the symptoms, lying down a lot. There are other, physical ones. A weakness inside you, just like an aching in your bones, especially your legs, around the knees. Another symptom is something I call 'burning eyelids'; I shut my eyes and it's as if I've got two hot coals instead of eyelids. And then there's a pain that rises from my left eye up across my forehead, catching me on the ridge above my eyebrow before it spreads over my whole head and gradually goes away as it moves down towards my neck. And a constant sick feeling in the pit of my stomach, I've got that too. I don't take anything for it, no medicine or anything. It's no good, I know that this isn't a physical disease.

When I touch my body and feel it getting flabby, I jump up and start walking around the room. I do fifty press-ups until my chest and arms are firm again. That's during the day, because I can't stand the noise of car horns in the street. In the evenings I go out for a stroll. I like watching the whores, the transvestites and the rent boys on the street corners. I like it so much that sometimes I pay one of them, a boy or girl, to sleep with me. That was how I got to know the Bar. But I don't want to talk about that now.

So I don't have to talk about that now, I lift my head, look away from the mirror to avoid seeing my dirty-looking bearded face and ever so slowly I loosen my grip on the basin and stare straight at my reflection in the mirror. I imagine that same guy on the circus tightrope, but the feel of the wire against the skin on the soles of his feet must be as cold and sharp as a knife blade. The edge of the basin is cold too, but round, round like a woman's breast or her arse. There's still nothing at all under my bare feet. I release my fingers from the basin and walk to the door to check the mail.

It's like that every day, several times a day, from two o'clock in the afternoon onwards. The landlady who rents me this room usually puts the letters on the little hall table. Often I open the door and peep out, but there's never anything for me. There couldn't be, of course, after all. I haven't got anyone left down in Passo. Only Dudu. And I'm not really sure whether now, after seven years, he's still mine forever or whether instead he'll never be mine again.

I didn't want to think about Dudu now, but when I opened the door and saw the hall table empty – empty of letters, I mean, because there's always that pink elephant with the plastic flower next to it – I couldn't help thinking, how nice it would be if I had a letter from Dudu now. Then I'd pick up the letter, sit down, read it slowly, there'd be news of Passo, it would talk about that little beach in September, about those afternoons when it was just getting warm again and we could start sunbathing again, me and him, because apart from me he was the only guy who knew that place. I'd light a cigarette and read on, then I'd take a pen and paper, think for a bit and begin my reply. After the date I'd have to write something, that was where I'd get stuck, unsure what would be best, whether *my-dear-Dudu* or *dear-Dudu, Dudu-my-friend* or just *Dudu*, or maybe *my friend*. I'd sit there for ages like that thinking, chewing the pen top, until it began to get dark. Maybe I'd decide to start writing without a date or anything, so as not to tell him everything. Maybe I'd leave the letter just like that, just a date on a blank page and I'd have a shower, shave and be done with it, then I'd slowly get dressed until it was time to go out to the Bar, deciding there was no need for any letter at all, not this time.

Except that that was the kind of thing I just didn't want to think about halfway through that afternoon when it was beginning to get dark. About Passo, the Bar, Dudu. All of that stuff's so bad for me.

I shut the door and leaned my forehead against it. People only do that in films, I've never seen anyone actually do it. I started to do it to see if I felt what people feel in films. People always feel things in films, in bars, on street corners, in songs, in stories. In real life too, I reckon, except they don't realise it. Then I noticed that the pain that shoots up from my left eye across my forehead was relieved slightly in that position, so I gradually turned round so that the left side of my head, where the pain was, was pressing against the closed door. There was less pain like that, although it wasn't exactly a pain. More a heaviness, a chill. A memory, a shame, a guilt, a regret that you can do nothing about.

I was standing with my back against the door when I looked out of the open window on the other side of the room. Then I thought, it would just take a quick run from the door to the window, then just the slightest push to throw my body through it and crash! whoa, that's it, over – I live on the tenth floor. It wasn't the first time that went through my mind. What held me back this time, as it did every other time, was thinking about that pile of trashcans down there in the yard. My little body, covered in hair and firm muscles, would fall right on top of them. I imagined some spaghetti leftovers tangled up in the locks of my curly hair, an empty bottle of cheap rum wedged between my legs, a used tampon on the end of my nose. And I stood still. I can't stand the thought of getting dirty, even after I'm dead.

3

Except that this time, Dudu, even with all the disgusting stuff I can imagine all over my body after it landed there, I don't know why, I still feel like jumping. But I'm fighting it. Not that anyone would miss me much or feel, I dunno, pissed off about my death. Not Teresângela, that little tart who came and gave me head four or five times, I think I told you about her, or Marilene, the Indian's wife, from Passo (give her my love), who was fond of me, so long ago, or the owners of the Bar, the little fat guy who smiles and sometimes waves from a distance, or the one with the moustache and the Charlie Chaplin bowler hat. Not anyone, Dudu. I began to count on my fingers the people who might miss me and there were plenty of fingers left over. All these ones I'm looking at now. I'm really unhappy Dudu and, here's a secret for your ears only, ever so slowly, right here inside, silently and secretly, I've been realising that I don't much like living any more, understand?

It's not that I'm short of cash. You can get by here. One day I sell books, the next I do some research. I dunno, something always turns up. I've never needed much, you know that. My only luxury has been thé Dulce Veiga records I scour the shops for, I've got nearly all of them, you'd enjoy hearing them, the other day I even found Dulce Says No Too, *signed and everything. I'm not short of love either, I told you about Teresângela, and there's Carlos too, over from Roosevelt Square, for when I drink too much, smoke dope, pop pills, forget myself and go kind of femme, plus there's Noélia, a reporter chick from* Bonita *magazine who I met in the Bar one night when she asked me my sign in the Chinese horoscope, I'm a Tiger and you, I remember, are a Dragon.*

Bittersweet love, of course, drunken love, end-of-the-evening love, street-corner love, love for money, shop-soiled love, lice in your pubes and disease, late-night Saturdays in this town you don't and won't ever know. Anyway, it's still love, Dudu, even if it doesn't quench your thirst. A helluva lot of love, on every corner, on every intersection, in every toilet. It's not that, or the lack of it. What's eating away inside me is something else, only you could know what, but even you didn't know back then and now I don't know whether I could explain it to you or to anyone else.

But what I want to tell you and I've only got a kind of vague idea because it just happened today, is something so crazy I don't know how to begin. Maybe like this – did you know I saw you one night? Don't laugh, don't doubt me, don't think it was like when you really miss someone and you start to see them in other people, everywhere, from behind, from something in the way they walk, smile or turn their head. It was different. And it wasn't just a desire to see you that brought you back, it was you, Dudu. You just like you are or were, seven years ago. The way someone, even by mistake, can never be someone else.

It was the first time I went to the Bar – and you were the reason I went there – about three or four years ago. I was coming down Augusta Street when I saw you turn the corner by the fruit stall, smile at me, wave with your hand, chewing gum (spearmint, I could tell) as usual, then went through one of those big, old iron gates. I went after you, I didn't even know it was a bar. I got lost in rooms full of smoke and strange people, people talking a lot, very loudly, I went through doors, through archways, down steps and up again, and finally stopped at a big window that opened onto the street. Then I looked across and there you were on the opposite pavement under the awning of a car showroom, a lingerie shop or dentists', I can't quite remember which.

You weren't some vision on the other side of the street, Dudu. You weren't even dressed in white, you were wearing those faded jeans, a bit torn at the bum and right knee, with a white tee shirt, like the ones you used to wear, chewing the gum that I could tell was spearmint from miles off. It was you, Dudu, no doubt about it. I retraced my steps, through the cigarette smoke, past the harsh sounds of all the words those people were hurling about like balls in the air, past the bar, crossed that little hallway, and pushed aside the people crowded by the gate while you waited for me on the other side. Then I had to stop and let a trolley-bus go past, one of those that go up and down Augusta Street all the time. By the time it had gone, you'd disappeared again.

Crazy isn't it, Dudu?

I wandered around for a bit, unable to believe it, and ended up in Roosevelt Square. That was the night I first met Carlão standing in front of the Bijou cinema, where they were showing, I remember it so well, The Story of Adele H., *the kind of film you used to like. In the distance, his hands in his pockets, a cigarette in his mouth, chewing gum at the same time, he looked like you. That was just the first time I saw you.*

Since that night I've had this thing about going to the Bar, thinking that it was somewhere you used to go, like we'd go to the Agenor da Boca, down in Passo, to meet Marilene when she'd run away from the Indian with a couple of poems in her handbag. I saw you on other nights, Dudu, always in the Bar. It happens so suddenly and quickly that I can never say anything. Sometimes I'm at a table, nearly always with Noélia, and you come down the stairs as if you were heading towards the big room at the front. You always smile and wave to me. Then you disappear.

I've never talked about you to anyone. And I'm not going to. I wouldn't be talking about you even to you, if I hadn't realised today that, as well as it being seven years since I left Passo da Guanxuma forever, it's close to your birthday. That's why I'm writing to you after so long. And to stop that desire to jump out of the window and put an end once and for all to that longing for Passo where I'm never going back, to that crazy obsession with looking for you in the Bar nearly every night and not finding you. I miss you so much, Dudu.

Sometimes I think that, when I'm ready – although I haven't got the slightest idea what it's like to-be-ready – one day, an ordinary day, any old day, a day like today, I'm going to find you sitting pale and calm in the Bar waiting for me. At the table opposite with a glass of wine that you'll raise in the air like a greeting until I come over without you disappearing and give you a hug and a gentle thump on the shoulder, without hurting you, like I used to do, and sit down with you to tell you everything that's happened to me these seven years.

Since that just-warm September afternoon when we stretched out naked beside each other on the pale sand of the banks of the gully at Caraguatatá, on a day close to your birthday, the sky so blue it looked hand painted, those spring gales quickly drying our wet hair, as a yellow butterfly fluttered about us and flew off just at the moment when you leant across the sand to look deep into my eyes, then slowly stretched out your arm as if you wanted to touch me somewhere so hidden and dangerous that I couldn't allow your eyes on the curly hairs of my body, your hand on the skin that in those days wasn't white like now, your minty breath almost inside my mouth. It was then that I picked up one of those cold pebbles from the water's edge and crack! I hit your head a single blow with all the strength of my firm muscles – so that you would die at last and only after killing you Dudu could I run away from you forever, from myself and from that damned Passo da Guanxuma that I can't forget, however many stories I make up.

IX

Queen of the Night

'And I dream the dream that stretches on from one street to the next to the next in vain.'

(Lucia Villares: *Angel Talk*)

It's as if I was outside the movement of life. Life going round over there like a Ferris wheel with everyone inside and me sat here like a fool at the bar. Doing nothing, as if I'd unlearnt everyone else's language. The language they use to communicate with each other when they're going round like that, round and round on that Ferris wheel. You've got a pass for the Ferris wheel, a password, a code, I dunno. You say something like *bah* for example, then the guy lets you through, you sit down and go round with the rest of them. But I'm always stuck on the outside. Sitting here, not knowing the right word, can't even guess it. Watching from the outside, looking pissed off, dying to be up there going round with them on that stupid wheel – do you follow me, kiddo?

No, you don't understand a damn thing I'm saying. Queen of the night, they all call me that and they don't even know that I sleep all day. I can't stand the light and anyway I've never got anything to do. What? I make the odd note. That's right, I've got a scam going. I'm not going into detail and it's pointless insisting. Cheating, swindling, hustling. I've told you, it's pointless insisting, boy. I've learnt that if I go into detail, you're going to work out that I've got dough and if I've got dough you're going to want to have it off with me just because I've got dough. And it just so happens that I'm still enough of a stupid ridiculous fool to be looking for True Love. Stop laughing or I'll throw this glass straight in your face. I'll pay for the glass and the drink. I'll pay for the damage and even the bar if I feel like smashing it up. If I'm feeling randy and you're skint and I need a prick I'll buy yours, I'll pay for yours. How much do you want for it? Tell me and I'll pay. I'll pay for the drinks, the food and the bed. I'll pay for a fuck too, if necessary.

Squeeze it, of course I'll squeeze it for you. Don't worry, I'll squeeze it later. Is it a big one? I like them big, nice and thick. Not right now. Right now I want to talk about the wheel. The wheel, can't you see it, kiddo? It's over there, right there, going round. Look around you, dearie. Right next to you. At that chick there in black, the one with the spiky hair. All right, I know, at least two thirds of the people in this bar are wearing black and have got spiky hair, including us. Do you know something, if I'd thought ten years ago I'd be sitting here with you, I wouldn't have believed it. Black absorbs negative vibrations, I thought. The opposite to white, white reflects. But I reckon that what these kids are really after is absorbing, sucking right down to the evil core. What? Maybe I will, afterwards. No, it's all right. But I'm not talking about that at the moment, darling.

Don't you like me saying that? Oh, don't give me that, kid. If I'm buying the drinks, I'll say what I like, understood? I'll say *darling* just like that, just how I fancy. I'll say it again and again, darling-darling-darling. I'll grab your chin whenever I want and say it and repeat it over and over again darling-darling. Cleft chin, eh? I've noticed that men with cleft chins really like getting it up the arse. Have you had it up yours? For God's sake don't come on with one of those stories about how, one night, at somebody's place in Boiçucanga, you had to sleep in the same bed as a guy who blah blah. Every little bloke your age is dying to have it up the arse, *darling*. Cancer in the ascendant, I know, mooning about, with a plump little bum and your arsehole on fire. It's nothing to be ashamed of, it's in the stars, boy. Or else you really are a queer, so that's alright too.

Don't get up, I'll buy you another vodka, would you like one? Just so I can talk a bit more about the wheel. You're ever so young, you don't understand these things. Let life work away at your face first, then we'll... Oh sweetheart you know that's funny, I was going to say your *soul*. Shall I say it? OK, if you insist, I can. I wonder if I still can, how did it go again? Let life work away at your soul first, then we'll talk. Leave it until you're gone thirty, thirty-five, reaching forty and haven't got married and don't have any of those horrible creatures they call *children*, or a house of your own or any fucking thing. Wake up in the middle of the afternoon with a hangover, look at your worn-out face in the mirror. Alone at home, alone in the city, alone in the world. It's going to hurt so much, kid. Oh how I wish I had a warm old-fashioned heart and could cuddle you to my breast and spare you all that pain and torment that's coming. How I wish I could give you a warning – take the left-hand path, boy, because along the right-hand path there are these evil wolves and a terrible terrible loneliness.

The wheel? No, I don't know whether it's you who chooses. Take a good look at me – do I look like someone who's ever chosen anything in her life? By the time I realised, everyone had learnt that little password by heart and they were well away, safe in their little seats going round on the wheel. Except for me, except for me. If you're going round on the wheel you're happy. If you're not you're fucked. Just like me, do you think I look really fucked up? I know I do a bit but tell the truth, *really* fucked up? Wrong, I *have* got a few friends. Fucked up just like me. I prefer not to go around with them, they're no good for me. People my age, with the same sort of, I was going to say *problems*, sheer force of habit, there's no problem. You know what I mean, it's a drag. Just like a mirror. I look at their fucked up faces and there's my own fucked up face spat out back at me. Some of them go round on the wheel, but in a fucked up sort of way. They don't go round like you. You're so innocent, such a little clown in your Mr Wonderful tee shirt. Innocent because you don't even know you're innocent. My fucked up friends don't realise they aren't any more. There are things that you gradually, slowly, ever so slowly stop being and you don't notice. By the time you've realised, it's gone, that's it. That's what being young means, did you know that? You don't know anything. You're going round on the wheel as well, shall I prove it? All those people in black with spiky hair are smiling at you because you're the same as them. If there's going to be a party, they'll let you in on it, even if they don't know you. That's what going round on the wheel means, darling.

Not me they wouldn't. No smiles. Not a single knowing look. I'm not the same as them, they know that. Queen of the night they call me, I know. That is when they're not calling me something much shittier than that, because queen of the night's actually quite nice, I think. That sickly-smelling flower that only smells at night, you know the one? Like fuck you do. You were born in an apartment, watching the telly. You don't know anything apart from stuff like video, punk, gothic, computers, heavy metal and all that crap. You know what, sometimes I actually feel more sorry for you and those spiky-haired kids in black than I do for me and those fucked up friends of mine? There was a time when it looked like it was going to work out for us. It was going to, it was, do *you* know when it will? You haven't even got that. We had the illusion, but you came along after they killed our illusion. Everything was dead by the time you were born, boy, and I was already an old tart by then. So I feel sorry for you. I reckon I'm better than you lot, just because I grabbed it while it was still alive. OK, sorry, kid. No, not better. I was luckier, was that it? I got here first. And I even wonder too whether I'm not lucky being on the outside of that crappy wheel that's going round without ever stopping, without me. Deep down, it makes me sick, what about you?

You haven't seen anything, you haven't even seen love. How old are you, twenty? You look like twelve. You were born clutching a condom, scared to death of catching Aids. The deadly virus, pal, the love virus. You took it up the bum, you screwed some arse, and that's it – total paranoia. A week later a spot appears on your face and it's panic stations, Emilio Ribas Hospital here we come. The shits, a dry cough, swellings all over. Oh boy, they've really screwed up your little mind, right? You can't even kiss on the mouth without getting scared shitless. You read somewhere it's passed on from saliva. You can't even stroke someone's damp chest without holding on to your arse. You read somewhere it's passed on from sweat. Assuming you do read, of course. Tell auntie now, do you read, darling? No, you don't read anything. You see it on the telly, I know. But you get it on the telly too, the whole time – love kills love kills love kills. You can even catch it being next to someone, drinking out of the same glass. Have you ever thought whether I had it? Me, who's had it away with half the town and what's more I love queers.

I'm the queen of the night who's going to contaminate you with her poisonous deadly perfume. I'm the carnivorous nocturnal flower who's going to make you dizzy and drag you to the bottom of her putrid garden. I'm the cursed queen who's mercilessly going to pollute you and infect your blood with every kind of virus. Beware of me – I'm the deadly queen. Have you ever licked a woman's cunt? Of course not, I know, it might be fatal. Or a man's cock, fatal too. Have you ever smelt that damp smell people have in their crutch when they take their clothes off? It's written all over your face, everything you haven't seen or done is written on your face. You were born wearing a mask. You were born forbidden to touch another person's body. You can wank, I know, but it's that thirst for another body that sends us crazy and starts to kill you little by little. You don't know what it's like, that taste that makes you stay outside the wheel that's going round and round and it can fucking well go on going round forever for all I care, because the people going round on it are the people who manage to pretend they haven't seen what they've seen. Oh boy, the whole of this filthy world is weighing down on you, much more than me – and I haven't even started talking about death...

Have you ever seen someone dead, boy? It's ugly, boy. Death is very ugly, very dirty, very sad. I really wish I could be kind and tender and powerful and grant you eternal life. I wish I was a rich and noble queen who could lock you in the tower of her castle and save you from that inevitable meeting with death. Have you ever been face to face with it? I have, lots and lots of times. I've been through it, darling. I can read it in your face that you never have. That little queer's dimple in your chin, those little green eyes looking at me just like I was Isabella Rossellini taking a beating and begging *eat me eat me*, all grovelling and gorgeous. That dizziness you're feeling isn't because you're pissed. It's the giddiness of sin, darling, the dizziness of poison. What are you going to say at school tomorrow, eh? Yes, because you must be still going to school, with your lunch box and everything. I know – I met a girl, a bit past her prime, and she couldn't give a shit. Imbecile, you imbecile, poor angel imbecile stuck at the end of it all. That lovely little prick hidden there between your wings, that's all you've got for now. A lovely little prick, not a mark on it. All nice and pink. A real humdinger. Because I bet you haven't even had it go limp on you yet. You wake up with your cock as stiff as a board, anything makes you randy, even a keyhole. How many times a day? Well done, congratulations, you've come of age. But make a note for when you come down to earth in the future – no one ever quenches that thirst. Sex is in the mind, you'll never do it. Sex is only in your imagination. You get off on what you imagine makes you come, not a real person, understood? You always get off on what's in your mind, not the person you're in bed with. Sex means lies, sex means craziness, sex means being alone, boy.

I've become tired. I'm past it. How old? Oh, you won't believe me, forget it. The main thing is that you go in one ear and out the other, get it? You don't stay there, you don't leave a mark. I know I'll stay in you, I know I'll leave a mark on you. A deep mark. I know that in a while, when you're going round on the wheel, you'll remember that one night you sat down beside a crazy bitch who told you things, who talked to you about sex, loneliness, death. It's ugly, death's so ugly, boy. You go kind of green, did you know that? Almost the same colour as this cold spinach sauce. A bit lighter, but that's not the worst of it. There's something that's not there any more, that's the saddest thing. You look and look and look and their body becomes just like a chair. A table, an ashtray, an empty plate. Something with nothing inside. Just like the husk of a peanut thrown on the sand, that's how you go when you die, right boy? What about you, have you found out that you're going to die one day too?

Of course you can have it. You've got all nervous, do you want a cigarette? But you don't even smoke, what? Yes I do, I do understand, I always understand, I'm a very understanding woman. I'm so fantastically understanding and everything that if I take you to bed with me now and tomorrow morning you've stolen all my dough, you needn't think I'll think you're a bastard. Isn't that the height of understanding? I'll think that that's just your way, a kid stealing from a woman who's a bit spaced out, a bit past it, who's messed around with his little imbecile's angel head stuck out at the rotten stinking end of it all. That's fine, that's the way things are, ca-pi-ta-list, in gothic neon letters. A spaced out woman who's a bit past it just like me is bound to be robbed by a stupid randy little kid like you. Just so she'll stop being such a fool, falling into that trap of sex again.

Hang it, I'm starting to feel dizzy. That wheel spinning endlessly round and round. Take a good look. Who's going round on it? The young girls who want to get married, the young lads who are after some money to buy a car, the little executives after power and dollars, the couples who are sick of each other, but holding on to something. Being outside the wheel means not holding onto anything, not wanting anything. Like me – I'm holding on to fuck all, I don't want anyone. Not even you. No I don't, boy. If I want you, I can have you. After all, it's only a matter of one less cheque in the book, cheaper than a pair of shoes. But I'd rather have what I can't buy. And it's not you I'm waiting for, I told you. That someone's going to come through that door one day maybe, without any warning. Different from all these people dressed in black with spiky hair. If I want I'll fantasise and imagine him in a gabardine cape, with a wet hat, a two-day-old beard, cigarette in the corner of his mouth, real *film noir* stuff. But that's out of the movies, he isn't. I don't know what he's like yet, because I haven't even seen him. He's going to look right at me. He's going to sit down at my table, look me in the eye, take hold of my hand, rest his warm knee against my cold thigh and say, come with me. He's the reason I come here nearly every night, boy. Not you, or the others like you. I'm keeping myself for him. You can laugh at me but I'm only sitting here drunk, stupid, ridiculous, because in the middle of all this crap I'm looking for True Love. Beware of me – one day I'll find him.

Just because of him, this guy who hasn't come yet, I'm leaving you this money now, no, you don't need to give me any change, I'll take my bag and get the hell out. It's almost getting light, boy. The queens of the night gather in their perfume with the light of day. Alone in the shadows they poison themselves with crazy fantasies. Share that stupid youth of yours with that chick beside you, darling. I'm going off on my own. I've got a dream, I've got a destiny, and if I crash the car and smash my head in leaving here, everything's still going to be all right. Outside the wheel, riding on my craziness. Sitting there stupid, ridiculous, couldn't give a shit, solitary, poisonous. Post-everything, you know what I mean? Ultra-gothic, ultra-modern, pure sham. Hand me my jacket, boy, it's bloody freezing out there and when it gets to this hour of the night my spell wears off. I turn back into what I am every day, shut in alone and lost in my room, far from the wheel and everything: a frightened kid.

X

Honey and Sunflowers (to the music of Nara Leão)

1

Just like in that story by Cortazar – they met on the seventh or eighth day of tanning. The seventh or eighth because it was magical and right that they should meet, like Libra and Scorpio, exactly at that point where the I encounters the Other. In short, they met on the day when the white colour of urban skin begins to give way to golden brown, red gradually fades to gold and then teeth and eyes, green from so much gazing at the endless sea glint like those of felines peering through the undergrowth. And they looked at each other through the undergrowth. At that point when skin ingrained with salt begins to long for light silks, simple cottons and white linen and when the contemplation of one's own naked body reveals shadowy patches of hair which the sun hasn't reached. These patches shine phosphorescent in the dark, longing for other similar patches on other skins at the same point of transformation. And around the seventh or eighth day of tanning, running one's hands over these golden brown surfaces arouses a certain solitary pleasure, almost a perverse one, were it not such a mild thing, the pleasure of finding one's own flesh wonderful.

They looked at each other across the palm trees – carnivorous, but sated and therefore calm – for the first time.

Animal-like in the midst of the shadowy undergrowth they looked at each other and the blue sky suddenly grew round and satiny, and the green sea became a semi-precious stone. She was floating beyond the breakers where the foam from the waves won't bother you if you feel like just contemplating your feet as they blend into the white sand on the sea bed. Her eyes closed, lying on her back in the water in a black swimsuit, her hair spread about her, her hands apart, her legs apart as if she were making love with the sun. Only her closed mouth betrayed a certain hardness, but that mouth opened with a start when he came swimming from the shore, his head buried in the water, and unintentionally bumped into her.

That was how it happened. She was floating there her arms and legs spread wide open, travelling further than those ships which cross the horizon at dusk, bound no one knows where. Then he came along, first one arm and then the other, a bit clumsy, a bit wild, and suddenly as one arm stretched out in front of the other, the hand belonging to this arm, unintentionally and therefore a little roughly, touched her thigh. The girl shrank back like a wounded sponge, thrust out her chest and opened eyes that were a little bloodshot from the salt, the sea and the light. His hand shrank back too and they both lay there looking each other straight in the eyes, soaking wet, at just about midday under a roasting sun at the height of summer. You know what I mean, the startled look of a jaguar, a leopard in that gaze which, apart from him or her, took in only the open seas. Then he spoke,

'Sorry.'

'That's all right,' she said

They spoke as if they hadn't been startled. Hypocritically, sociably, two people spending a fortnight's holiday on some beach in Hawaii or Itaparica smiled amicably at each other beneath their drenched hair and pretended that everything was fine. And it was, I mean it. He swam off. She carried on floating. Indifferent, both of them. Swimming far off towards those sailing boats that weren't real but part of a seascape in a rather kitsch drawing, just the kind I'm sketching for you now. He looked back and saw her just as she was before, only artificially now, since he'd seen her: her eyes closed, arms and legs wide apart, abandoned as if she were making love with the sun. As he swam off, a bit clumsy, a bit wild, first one arm then the other, his face buried in the water, she too opened one eye and sneaked a look. He was swimming far away from her, a stone in the middle of the road, she thought, because, oh yes, she'd read a thing or two. But a stone, she imagined, that she would push aside with the toe of her shoe, if her feet weren't bare and submerged in the water. She wriggled her bare toes in the warm water. A cliché, a tropical dream – isn't it wonderful to be alive?

2

They met again the same evening. This time it was different. He lingered a bit longer in front of the mirror, drawing the white shirt and light blue trousers, quite baggy both of them, over his showered body. But he certainly didn't think of her or of anyone else as he looked at himself, I can assure you. Then he went to dinner in the hotel restaurant, salad things decorated with bananas and pineapples, macaws and toucans perched on top of soufflés, 'B' movie stuff, or even 'C' movie stuff, and if there had suddenly been a quick number with Carmen Miranda on the staircase it wouldn't have surprised anyone. She didn't take long. A city girl with a loyalty to black, she threw the silk blouse over her old, slightly torn jeans and only held out some sort of promise – promise of what, she couldn't honestly say at that moment – when she added a little string of pearls, hardly visible. Then she threw her hair to one side in a quick feminine gesture, so feminine that it's a favourite of transvestites.

Then they went down to dinner. Only in a manner of speaking, because, that's right, there weren't any stairs. Besides, we shouldn't exaggerate. They were like bungalows set side by side and to get to the restaurant you went along a kind of verandah-corridor covered with folksy fishing nets and hammocks strung between arched columns. If you really must know, yes there were straw baskets, stuffed fish hung on the whitewashed walls, alongside large strategically scattered ceramic pots – which inevitably reminded you of Ali Baba. And there were bare-chested brown-skinned guys too, in white trousers, lying in hammocks playing the guitar. And brown-skinned girls with flowing hair and printed dresses with tiny flowers, walking so naturally amongst the pots that it all seemed real. That rustic bit, all of them brown, glowing, panting, ecological, employed by the hotel. They came walking along this corridor, him in white, her in black, until they entered what was called, somewhat pompously and only moderately convincingly, The Great Hall.

They didn't meet straight away. She sat at a table on the left, with The Secondary School Teacher Recovering From Her Bitter Separation, The Executive Secretary Dying For An Affair With Those Gorgeous Hunks and The Old Maiden Aunt Tired Of Looking After Her Nephews. He sat down at a table on the far right – nothing ideological there – next to The Couple In The Middle Of Their Hard-Won Second Honeymoon and The Basketball Player Looking For A More Natural Life. Chatting over the prawn soufflé and champagne punch, for it was a five star hotel, she did quite well to quote Ruth Escobar, Regina Duarte, an article from *Nova* magazine and even ventured into Susan Sontag, but no one got that one. Meanwhile he screwed up his second empty pack of Marlboros and was a bit too lazy to defend Paulo Francis but agreed that the ministries, whether for culture or for sport or education, weren't about that at all. When all was said and done, he did miss the old Aero Willys, the *made-in-Brazil* automobile.

They did come face to face when it was time for the dessert of grated coconut with mashed banana. This time she was the one who bumped into him. He looked at her then with that rather weary look of someone who's enduring an extremely boring evening in order to see a girl he'd seen once before. With her hair tied back wearing a black silk blouse with torn jeans, she was a girl who looked as though she'd been trapped into having to endure an extremely boring evening and he only vaguely remembered that he knew her from somewhere. But she spotted in that dark man, his nose peeling a bit on the end, precisely the guy who had bumped into her on the beach except that his hair was dry and he was dressed. She smiled, because she had slightly provocative impulses like that, and said,

'Now we're quits.'

Rather stupidly, as men tend to be whether they're on holiday or not, he grunted,

'Unh?'

And it was when she said excuse me and he moved back a bit, that, seeing her from behind, her back was too straight, a little tense, he recognised the-floating-girl and said,

'How are you ?'

'Great,' she replied.

Then they helped themselves to food, ate, got slowly bored through the evening, which didn't take too long – unless you wanted to wade through oceans of daiquiri and then, and you could too, call up one of those boys in the white trousers, without the guitar of course, or one of those girls in the printed dresses. Then start a little affair that would leave you with one less cheque in your book and, who knows, some kind of sweaty and one would hope absolutely – or at least slightly – wild pleasure. They didn't want to. On that night, at that moment in time, in this story, definitely not. They looked

distractedly at each other from afar, had their coffee, smoked
their cigarettes, said excuse me, leaned for a while out over
the verandahs to the sound of It's-so-lovely-to-die-at-sea or
My-raft's-going-out-to-sea. Then they discreetly went to bed.
Alone.

3

Before going to sleep he smoked three Marlboros. She took
half a sleeping pill. He leafed through a biography of Dashiell
Hammett, poor bugger, he thought and was Lilian Hellman
really such a viper? Then he put out the light, turned over,
tried to lie there with a stiff cock between the sheets which,
he thought, smelled of seaweed, but seaweed doesn't smell of
anything, something green then; he fell asleep halfway
through a half-hearted wank. She opened a Margaret Atwood
book, but what a slow business, all that caper about women
dressed in red, then something by Doris Lessing, but that was
a bit disgusting with all that stuff about the old woman living
in a basement, then she put out the light and unintentionally
thought Carlos, but it no longer brought back anything not
even a sign of emotion; then she fell asleep nestled in her own
sunburnt skin. How wonderful & restful, they both thought
just before they fell asleep.

The next morning, as she was laying out her towel, a giant
fleecy dollar bill, she peeped out from beneath her pussy-cat
sunglasses every which way, not that she was looking for
someone, until, nothing planned or anything, she spotted
him a few yards away. A man with a bit of a belly, true,
nothing serious, but broad shoulders, strong legs, hands on
his hips, daringly alone. He was looking at her, quite by
coincidence. She gave a Pavlovian smile. He raised his hand.
She too raised her hand. Hanging there like that in the air,
for a moment his hand and hers were saying something like

hi, so you're here. Something like that, nothing to do with anything. Meticulously, conscientiously, she rubbed the *urucum* lotion on her skin and then lay down with her back to the sun. While he, without any lotion or oil, lay face down on the bare sand (with so many parasites and fungal spores, my God), because men are like that, she thought, so rough. And she felt a shiver. It was in that shiver that she realised.

He realised when, lying face down, beneath the synthetic fabric of his black trunks, his cock stiffened. He slowly moved his bottom about, without anyone noticing, in an in-and-out motion, you know, sort of fluidly. Meanwhile, they looked at each other. She from behind her pussy-cat sunglasses; he behind his frowning eyebrows, behind his eyelids shut tight because of the increasingly strong sun. Sideways glances, each of them in their own way beginning to realise.

A big black guy came round selling things. He got a can of beer and she thought that was a bit crude. She had a lemon juice and he thought that was chic, even in a plastic cup. Then she almost fell asleep in the increasingly hot sun, a few memories mingled with fantasies, and she was actually going to resist the urge to sleep when she saw the Executive Secretary coming across in a Stunning Tiger-stripe Bikini and she decided instead to sink once and for all into that sweaty nonsense which brought back to her a man's name, a certain bitterness or other, feelings of fright, flashbacks, her in a navy blue pleated skirt, a schoolmistress with a huge nose saying you'll go far, my girl. She *was* going far – to Madagascar or Bali, where she would write a definitive book about The Wisdom Gained By Western Women After Their Great Disillusionment With Everything Including Men.

Suddenly, she sensed something had happened in her field of vision and she opened her eyes. Bathed in sweat, dazed like that girl in a navy blue pleated skirt, books pressed to her small breasts. Between two hairy muscular male thighs, she first saw the crest of the sea and a surfer riding the waves but as if the scene were framed by what, only after a while, wiping her brow, did she realise were two male thighs. She looked at him: 'Eh?'

He was standing there beside her. His left hand on his hip, his right shading his eyes from the sun, he was looking at her. The woman, not all that young, stretched out on her back on a white towel, facing the sun. When he realised she was looking at him, he bent his knees and gradually crouched down until he was almost at her level. A bit clumsily, a bit too obviously, but it was summer and without anything really to talk about and not quite knowing why, he asked,

'How's it going?'

'Fine', she said. 'How about you?'

4

They chatted on the eighth or ninth day. They swam together down by the beach and when she got thirsty, he bought her another lemon juice and had another beer. Lying on the sand next to each other, they talked. If you want me to tell you, I'll repeat it all but it's nothing original I can assure you. She was something like a Psychologist Who Dreamed Of Writing A Book; he was something like a Senior Banking Executive Who Feels Like Leaving It All Behind To Live On A Boat Like the Emir Klink Who Crossed The South Atlantic Solo. She, who hardly smoked, accepted a cigarette. And said that she liked Fellini. He agreed, out of this world. To her surprise he talked about Fassbinder. She went further and countered with Wim Wenders. He then got a bit frightened, retreated and tried to stall her with Bergman. She said oh, but pressed on further and made a radical move with Philip Glass. He said I didn't see the show, and started to expound upon minimalism, one-nil to him. She took the opportunity to make a long, somewhat tense digression about something like Identities

Between Minimalist Aesthetics And The Bossa-Nova Feeling. He listened in amazement, one-all.

At one-all they came together over João Gilberto, whom they both listened to alone in their small but well-appointed apartments in the city when they felt like turning on the gas, throwing themselves out of the window or slitting their wrists, and there was no one there in the small hours. They got so in tune together that, past noon, she also said yes to a beer. A little silly but very happy, they started singing *The Birdie Song*, while all those Athletes Willing To Do Anything For A More Perfect Body, Gays Running Away From The Urban Paranoia Of Aids, Elderly Ladies But Still All There, and so on disappeared in search of their lunch. The sun was scorching, scorching hot. Then he saw a little boat gliding across the soft blue of the sea, showed her, she saw it too and they pointed and laughed and the sun didn't seem so intense – it was the eighth or ninth day of tanning. That day when the brown has taken over your skin and you can take off your sunglasses without fear, just as she did, to look at him straight in the eyes. Which smiled. Everything was so tropical, they were on holiday, they killed themselves laughing, said see you, no hurry, as they said goodbye at the bungalow door, hers was number 19, he fixed it in his mind. And they each went off to have their freshwater shower.

They found out in the evening, dancing to *Love is a Many Splendoured Thing*. At first a little apart, then closer and closer as the bandleader struck out along perilous paths such as the Beatles, Caetano Veloso or Roberto Carlos. They sang *Eleanor Rigby* together, they were both over thirty and she suddenly got goose pimples hearing I'm-gonna-ride-the-whole-night-through and leaned her head on his shoulder. He squeezed her waist harder. And on they went like this, going giddily round and round, occasionally sitting down to talk about Pessoa, Maisa or Clarice Lispector. Gradually finding out, pinning down, laying siege.

He was trying to forget a woman called Rita. As the whisky went down in the bottle, Rita gradually merged with someone else called Helena, he repeated how-I-loved-that-woman-never-again-never-again, while she felt some hatred but didn't say anything, repeating ever so maturely it'll-pass-just-a-matter-of-time-it'll-be-fine. To his surprise, she spoke the name of that man from before, and others too, Alexandre, Lauro, Marcos, Ricardo – ah, men called Ricardo, none of them are any good – and he too felt a certain hatred, nothing serious, just normal, modern times, simply two cheated lovers meeting. Then they talked about passions, deceptions, needs and all those things that happen in people's hearts and everything, and nothing. They danced again. He thought it was so nice resting his face on that curve in her neck. She thought it was a bit much to be showing off like this with a man, who was after all a stranger, resting his face on her neck like that but she pressed her groin harder and harder against his – pelvis, pelvis, she repeated, rehearsing the dance steps in her head one-and-two-and-three – such a forlorn, neat and tidy man smelling of Paco Rabanne or Eau Sauvage, or was it Phebo? She didn't know. The smell of a proper, decent man and fuck it; after all, they were on holiday. And free, but that damned virus means you have to be careful. She let his hand slide down below her waist. And at a louder beat from the percussion, as they twirled, spinning round together, she asked him,

'Let me look after you.'

'OK', he said.

5

They went on like that for the few days that remained. Four or five, less than a week. They'd walk barefoot on the sand at night by the sea shore – I swear it. Slowly their hands would touch; yours are so long, yours so square. He didn't want to get involved in another affair because it was too painful. She didn't want to get involved in another affair because it was too painful. She had assumed her destiny as a Totally Liberated But Profoundly Misunderstood Woman Who Accepted Her Inevitable Solitude. He was absolutely certain about his choice of an Independent Man Who Can Do Without That Nonsense Called Love. And so they walked and walked, remembering bossa nova lyrics together. She imitated Nara Leão: if-someone-asks-after-me. He imitated Dick Farney: you're-the-dawn-chorus-of-life. They knew nothing of punks, goths, new romantics. They were so old, walking hand in hand along that sparkling sand, soft under the feet as they slowly sank into it. Lobster flesh, cream, snow. So nice meeting you, finding a quiet spot, with a guitar.

Later they'd kiss just a little too ardently at the door of her bungalow. Or his, when he drank too much and couldn't stand up on his own but that was tolerable, if frequent. Only about three times on the mouth. The moon was so full, they were so timid. Only once with their tongues. A little self-consciously; he had a permanent bridge on the upper right side while she had a pin holding in a premolar on the lower right side. He thought her so dignified & superior, she thought him so elegant & respectful. And they thought; this is just a holiday romance, it won't lead anywhere, it's just a way of passing the time. If he'd had friends around, they'd say just give her one, you're going to score there, mate. If she'd had friends around they'd play at being the witches of Eastwick, they'd discuss smells, sizes, they'd check up on her cheque stubs. In actual fact there was no one else there, he'd leave her or she'd leave him. That was it, then they'd go to bed. And they'd dream about each other in the five-star darkness of their bungalows with the parabolic aerials.

She lies on her back in bed, he thought, just in her knickers. She's got small breasts that he'd take in each of his hands, like someone holding two apples, little green apples. I lie on top of her and nestle my head on her shoulder. She runs her right hand down my back, licks my ear, runs her hand further and further down my back – scratching without hurting, she's got short nails – to just above my bottom, then she starts to pull down my pants, I can feel my chest pressed against her little breasts as she carries on ever so slowly pulling down my pants and then I start to feel the pressure of my cock against her navel until my pants reach my knees and I press my cock against her belly, then she says sweetheart-sweetheart, and when my pants reach my ankles I kick them off into the middle of the room and lie completely naked against her, she's completely naked too because I slowly start pulling down her panties as I say: my mother, sister, wife, friend, whore, lover – I love you.

He gets on top of me, she thought, as I wait for him lying on the bed. He nestles on top of me like a baby who'd like to suckle my breast which I then lift up to him, offering him the hard nipple. He runs his hand down my back which I arch a little so that he can squeeze me around the waist, as I nestle further into his body and slowly pull down his pants until he kicks them off into the middle of the room at the same time as his hand around my waist has pulled down my panties and thrown them into the middle of the room. Then we press against each other completely naked, as he enters me, so gently, and tells me you're the woman I've always searched for all my life and I tell him you're the man I've always searched for all my life and we drown in each other and cover each other in saliva and smear each other in the saliva from our mouths and the liquid from our sex as I say: my father, brother, husband, friend, mate, enchanted prince – I love you.

6

At the end of the fortnight they were golden brown all over. They swam. He said, between strokes, that he was missing the Avenida Paulista, the rush hour, car horns, digital watches. They ate prawns. She said she was missing the Rodeo, sliced sirloin, watercress salad, dry martinis. They ran along the beach together without saying a word. But everything about every move they took seemed to say what a pity, baby, summer's over, picture postcards, click, that's it. They smoked cigarettes, drying off on the sand, watching the horizon, talking artificially about The Book She Was Going To Write and The Boat Where He Was Going To Live because after all they weren't animals, they respected each other's in-tel-lect. More than thirty years old, nearly ten in analysis, no ties, a bit of security, completely free. All that Fake-Hawaii around them; mature, ready. And waiting.

He offered her another Marlboro, which she accepted. She rubbed Coppertone on his back, and he let her. She said it was so good meeting you in the middle of all these mediocre types, and he smiled, proud of himself. He said I never thought I'd meet a woman like you in a place like this (but it isn't some whorehouse, she thought suspiciously) and she smiled, flattered. He stretched out his leg and his foot came right next to hers. Her foot was white, arched from so many years of dancing. His foot was brown with a prominent bunion, damaged nails, an executive's foot. As if by accident, his foot rested on top of hers. She let it stay there – the last day, there was no time left. The next morning, that's it – *the end*, without the *happy?* She felt a little giddy in all that sun and he asked whether she wanted some water. She suspected that he thought her a bit boring and past it because after all, during all those days she hadn't even attempted anything more. He suspected that she thought him a real square because during all those days he hadn't attempted anything more. They looked at each other with so much suspicion and understanding, after midday on the roasting hot beach. His eyes were watering in all that light. She lent him her pussycat sunglasses and then laughed as he put them on and made a camp pose. I wonder if he is, she thought. And she looked in such a determined way at the girls playing volleyball that he thought, I wonder if she is. Modern times, who knows. The sun was still going down, they had three cans of beer each, remembered all the words to darling-it's-a-year-and-a-half-since-our-home-fell-apart, she thought with displeasure of her green Fiat making its way through Minhocão at eight in the morning, he thought with displeasure of the three telephones on his desk and they both thought of all those things with such displeasure that they had another beer, the sun still going down. There was no one else left on the beach when they saw the crimson ball of the sun sinking into the sea over towards Japan. When it's dawn there, it's dusk here, he said. They vaguely arranged to have sushi on the Avenida da Liberdade. But it was the last day, the height of summer and they didn't fancy each other in the slightest, what a pity.

7

That evening they ate lobster. Her all in white, hair loose, golden brown from the sun, a little bleached from the salt. Him all in black, his shirt open at the chest, fresh skin peeling on the tip of his long nose. Then they danced, they always danced. They hardly said a thing. A warm breeze was blowing in off the sea, just like that, stirring the tops of the palm trees. I'm such a lonely woman, she said suddenly. I'm such a lonely man, he said suddenly. It was when the band began to play *Lygia*, by Tom Jobim, that they said together: João should record this some day, has he? I can't remember – and-when-I-fell-in-love-it-was-just-an-illusion. They held each other so tight, with nothing in mind, just carried away by it all, that they didn't notice the dance floor emptying, and suddenly it was three, nearly four in the morning. Her bus to the airport left at eight, his at nine and the two of them were still in the middle of the floor, they couldn't stop dancing to things like *Moonlight Serenade, or As Time Goes By*, their own secret tunes. They were so settled, so square and so wanting, they were so lost in the middle of that sub-Hawaiian fantasy that was coming to an end. She was just a girl wanting to write a book and he was just a boy wanting to live on a boat, but nourishing each other so they... So they could what? They didn't seem to have the slightest idea.

The smell of him on her hands when she went to bed, without him, was so nice. The smell of her on his hands when he went to bed, without her, was so nice. Her body melted so well into his when they danced. He liked it when she rubbed oil on his back. She liked it when, after she was silent for a long time, he took hold of her chin and asked, what's wrong, little girl? He liked it when she said, do you know what, I've never been able to talk to anyone like I have to you. She liked it when he said it's funny, you're like someone I've known for a long time. And when he said calm down, you're tense, come here, and held her in his arms and made her rest her head on his shoulder so she could look into the distance, at the horizon, until everything was better, and everything did get better like that. He liked it so much when she ran her fingers through the hair on the nape of his neck, those curly hairs, and said silly, you're just a silly boy.

Like the other evenings, he walked her to the door of bungalow 19, at nearly five in the morning, for the last time. But unlike the other evenings, she invited him in. He went in. So stark in there, despite being a five-star bungalow. He didn't know what to do so he stood near the door while she opened the window to let in the warm breeze from the sea. She suddenly seemed very sure of herself. She pressed a button and from a cassette player the voice of Nara Leão started singing. She came over to him swaying a little to the sound of the guitar and invited him to dance, just a little more. He accepted, just for a bit. He closed his eyes, she closed her eyes. They moved round and round, their eyes closed. For a long time, round and round, on and on:

'I won't forget you,' he said.

'Nor me you,' she said.

He moved her back a little, so he could see her properly. She shook her hair and looked him straight in the eyes. A sort of intoxication. Not just sort of, with all that vodka and pineapple. They stopped dancing. Nara Leão went on singing. The moonlight was shining in through the window. That warm breeze that they wouldn't have any more the next day. Then he saw her properly; a woman who was a bit too thin, somewhat tense, full of ideas, not very young – but so sweet. Her hands resting on his shoulders, brushing away her hair like that, in the same instant she saw him properly; a man who was not very tall, with a confused expression, a slight belly, not very young – but so sweet. What a huge trap, they thought. They stood there looking at each like this, nearly morning.

She couldn't bear looking that long. She turned round and leaned out of the window, a scene from a film, Doris Day, chaste but daring. Then he came up behind her, Cary Grant, gentle giant. He touched her slowly on her bare, golden-brown shoulder under the strap of her low-cut dress, and said,

'Do you know what, I've been thinking a lot. I reckon…'

She suddenly turned round. And said:

'Me too. I reckon…'

They stood there looking at each other. Golden brown all over, eyes moist. Was it the breeze? Midsummer rampant outside. Close to her, he asked,

'What?'

'Yes', she said.

She pulled him even closer to her, by the waist.

'You look like honey', he said.

'And you look like a sunflower', she said

They stretched their hands out to each other. With precisely the gesture of someone about to pick a perfectly ripe fruit.

XI
The Other Voice

It was five fifteen in the afternoon. He knew without even looking at his watch, he knew even though there was no sun that day, so he couldn't watch the usual bright patch of light steadily shrink on the wall opposite the open window as night fell. And they would come with the night. But he was afraid to think about that and so imagined that he knew by a kind of vibration in the air, as if things, those things outside, had a special movement of their own like a slight breathlessness, every day after five-fifteen in the afternoon. Except things weren't moving. Maybe they were, who knows, inside or on the surface of his body, a tightening of his bowels, a dilating of his pupils, a quickening of his heartbeat, tiny drops of sweat on the palms of his hands – a brief outbreak of panic in his soul.

In any case he knew, wherever the warning came from. He was so sure that – just like the other times – he put his hand on the phone just before it rang. And even before he'd started to wait, because it was five fifteen, he shuddered as he heard it ring, almost smiling to himself inwardly, because somehow it was as if the ringing was produced merely by the vibration of his fingers hovering over the receiver. If only he had the power to magnetise the other person's hand, forcing the forefinger of that other person's hand to dial his six or seven numbers and call him up. But now he didn't have any power, if he ever had done. And he reckoned he didn't, apart from this power he had now, of keeping the bridges intact for as long as necessary, however long that was.

He only answered the phone after it had rung three times.

It was bright and alive, the other voice, full of sharp crystals. Little fragments of crushed ice jangling against the edges of a glass. So gleaming that he was dazzled and couldn't help but blink. He looked out of the window and at the shadow on the wall opposite. He had to have time, in that transition between the darkness inside the cave and the electrified field of light. From inside that shadow zone, adjusting his corrupted retinas he slowly asked (even though he knew who it was), 'Who is it?' and repeated it twice, three times, until the voice stopped talking about something he couldn't quite make out, something or other from out there, intelligible only to someone who was out there, in the middle of what was living, without beginning or end and that wasn't particularly addressed to him, like an interruption from a crossed line:

'Don't you recognise me? It's still me.'

He held the phone a little away from his ear – the other voice was so loud. Not that it was unpleasant or too harsh. On the contrary, escaping from the little holes in the receiver the sound seemed to scatter into all the corners of the narrow room. It struck the walls in reflected echoes, spilled over all the objects, enveloping them in thin tissues of sound, dissolved the mustiness, filled the shadows with sun-drenched colour. A cicada's wing on a midsummer's morning. The dark room gleamed, coated in the brilliance of the golden voice. Please, he wanted to beg, take me away from here, I need help before it's too late. But that wasn't allowed. Strict solemn rituals, hidden behind the formulae of politeness at five-fifteen in the afternoon. And the pain like a moth-eaten hole concealed under a candlestick. He brought the receiver closer to his ear again, tenderly and carefully:

'What's wrong? Aren't you well?'

'I'm fine', he said slowly. He couldn't possibly say 'I'm afraid' or something like that; something personal, alarming. He lifted his free hand to his heart, and sighed, between two heartbeats, 'There's nothing wrong. I'm fine.'

'I got the impression you weren't listening.'

The voice like a river, water trickling over smooth bright pebbles, and a yellow flower, its corolla spattered with water, repeated the words, its rough stem scratching his own throat as it asked to be let out – and the telephone line linking the two voices across the city, at five fifteen in the afternoon:

'I need time'.

'What?'

'Time. I always need a little time, from the moment you start to speak before...'

The voice laughed. Slightly conspiratorially, almost tenderly, a frequent and willing visitor to the staircase inside him, the dust, the attics, some clinging cobwebs getting in the way and suddenly tripping over in the middle of a familiar corridor although he hadn't finished speaking:

'Before I can speak. It's my voice. It gets so that it's as if I don't have any control over it. Then it seems to come from a long way off, it's not mine. Hasn't that ever happened to you?'

'You can always sing. Or read a book aloud. Haven't you got any books there?'

'You know I haven't', he started to say. But the noise of an aeroplane or a car at the other end of the line interrupted the sound for a moment. A cloud covered the sun. There were noises there, and movements, tremblings, throbbings, he could feel them coming across the line, restless, almost alive, and emerging from the phone with the voice, writhing around the corners of the room. Nothing of interest apart from the bars on the window, which they would shy away from in disgust. That curious, pitying disgust felt for an animal in a cage.

'I want you to get better soon', the other voice said. And it seemed true. Just hearing it he felt like leaning out of the window to say hello to someone hanging out washing down below, without any fear of them snarling at him. There weren't any washing lines. On the other side of the window there was just the high concrete wall, the barren yard covered in paving stones, without any plants. And before that the bars, to block off in advance the leap he hadn't yet taken. (*At the other end the girl smiled, more with her blue eyes behind her glasses than with her small mouth with its well-defined, plump lips. The way she always smiled. He made a gesture in the air to help her – she'd been so hesitant lately, since she'd forgotten how to stand up and had lost interest in doing so, engrossing herself in the learning of other more delicate ways of balancing. She shunned him gently but firmly as if to say that it didn't matter now, any help is futile now I've made up my mind to make the crossing –* 'I hold you tight, I hold you tight and throw myself off'.) He wanted to repeat that line by Ana Cristina César down the phone and threaten the voice with some gentle blackmail. All he could say was,

'Thanks.'

Under the palm of his hand against his chest, under the cloth of his shirt, amongst the mass of flesh intertwined with muscles, nerves, fat, veins, bones, his heart was beating wildly. *You're going to abandon me*, he repeated soundlessly, his lips moving right by the receiver, *and I can't do anything about it. You're my only link, an umbilical cord, a bridge between here inside and there outside. I can see you disappearing every day amongst those living things where I am not present. I'm afraid of being more and more absent, day by day, from all that you see. And then, so much time will have gone by that everything will become routine and my absence will be of no importance. I'll be just a memory, it'll be a relief; whereas now I'm a carnivorous plant demanding a drop of blood every day to stay alive. You slowly slit your wrist with your own nails so that I can drink. But one day it will be too much effort, too much pain, and then you'll forget; the way one forgets a rather unimportant engagement. A half-bitten fruit rotting in silence on the plate:*

'Eh?'

'Nothing. I didn't say anything.'

'I got the impression I heard you talking. Very quietly. I thought you were talking to them.'

'Who?'

'You know. What is it you call them?'

'Ana, Carlos. They're not here at the moment.'

'Have they been back?'

'Every night.' (*Patient, determined, the boy waited for the party to end. So determined that, if someone watched him more closely, they'd no doubt notice a more definite shape to his movements, no longer at all hesitant, and perhaps something harder in his voice, a strange light in his eyes. The accounts had finally been settled and there'd been nothing left over. One by one, he waited for them all to leave. Later, in the empty house, he'd clean the ashtrays and gather up the crumbs of the party from the corners of the room the crumbs of the party and throw them in the bin. Maybe he'd look at the summer night, standing at the door, alone with the choice he'd made, and breathe very deeply, one more time, letting the heavy smell of the sea befuddle his weary brain, so weary of all those years of weariness. All so minute he hadn't even noticed them weighing down on him. He was slight and gentle in his movements and speech, as if he was afraid somehow of disturbing everyone else's vibratory field. He'd look at the things one last time, ordinary things: sofa, chair, table. Maybe not, he'd be utterly blind just as he took off each piece of clothing one by one. He'd be looking over to the other side, like someone who's climbing a hill and, nearly at the top, can just make out some shapes, a bush, some ant hills, purple patches of creeping flowers scattered along the path leading down. Slowly, slowly. Slow nakedness, then his fingers tying the knot. Then the gesture of pulling it over his head, like a crown – the crown of laurels he'd never had or had stopped waiting for – rather ridiculous, far too big, so that the rope slipped down scratching slightly the tip of his nose and his chin. He'd carefully adjust the knot at his throat, getting his tie ready for the party on the other side – would it be a party? He wouldn't say anything, although at night sometimes, when they came, he'd reveal certain fragmentary, incomplete words – in the vague code of those who have gone away – that disappeared forever into the world of forgotten dreams when he uselessly attempted to reconstruct them the next morning. But no, he wouldn't say anything. You don't say another word when everything has already been said, in many ways, but never clear enough to be understood by anyone else. Then the body jerks away, like someone about to take flight, as it hangs from the gallows. After that, on days that are too hot, the sea breeze mingles with the smell of rottenness and scatters it; a whiff of the sea wafting its stench of death and escaping between the curves of the sand on the dunes of the remote beach.):*

'Eh?'

'The trees, I said. The cinnamon trees, you know. Have they started giving off that sweetish smell?'

'I haven't noticed.'

'Well notice, then. Notice for me. Then tell me about it.'

'But you can't tell someone about a smell.'

'Explain it then. Will you?'

'I'll explain it and tell you all about it. But get rid of them.'

'Get rid of them, will you teach me how to?

(She'd arrive with the night too, the thin blonde girl with the fine hair of an Englishwoman. As the darkness stole into the room, the whiteness of her clothes became clearer, almost phosphorescent, always in the corner on the left lurking near the windows. They never came together. And he didn't know whether he was more frightened by his slowness or her haste. In either of them the act was all prepared. To execute it would simply mean carrying out directions that had long been rehearsed in their minds. With her there were three quite distinct moments, but so quick they might have seemed like just one if she didn't repeat them every night in

slow motion, one by one. First, the closed door. Next, the razor blade onto her wrist. When the blood began to flow and you could see a long trickle stretching red across her white clothes – then, at first glance, she looked like a little girl frightened by her first period. Between this moment and the other one there was that very short moment when she stood at the window, staring out. And like him, the other one who also used to come, he'd never know whether she was contemplating everything for the last time: the cars, the concrete streets shimmering in the heat, the pools of light, mirages, the dark heads of the people above their brightly coloured clothes and the pairs of legs underneath going to and coming from places where she would never go again, or whether she was looking beyond everything, to a place where she could maybe vaguely make out, blurred like a face behind glass on a rainy day, a pair of familiar eyes, a smile. No, no smile. Hard lips and eyes. The act of standing up on the parapet and the second before, they always seemed to be about to fly away. I hold you tight, *she repeated.* I hold you tight and throw myself off. *Then the leap, the fall, the sound of bones breaking, screams, the siren and people running across the dirty pavements of Copacabana.*):

'Come and see me one day', he said.

'You know it's not allowed.' Her voice of water or sunlight now seemed clouded over with a shadow, a shadow like weariness. Or so he thought at first, and then, more harshly; a kind of impatience, a distancing, a tiredness from always repeating the same things, at five fifteen in the afternoon:

'I'll be fine', he promised.

'Of course you will.'

'One day I'll come back.'

'Of course you will. Come and see the cinnamons.'

'It's not my fault.'

'Of course not.' 'They're getting vaguer and vaguer. Like those patches of mist you get in the mountains. On a winter's morning, when the sun's beginning to break through the clouds.' He'd started to lie, so intensely that maybe he was telling the truth. He could almost see them, with their bodies getting fainter and fainter as he spoke. 'They're getting thin, kind of transparent. Their voices are weaker and weaker. I can hardly understand what they're saying. They barely finish their movements, they're like ink drawings on wet paper. Fading away, but ever so slowly – I don't know how long I can stand it.'

'As long as it takes. I'll be here.'

'Maybe it's all up to me.'

'Everything has its time. There's their time too. I'm the bridge for you, you're the bridge for them.'

'I'm afraid you'll fail me. Because, if you fail, so will I. And I can't.'

'I'm not going to fail you. Not because I can't, but because I don't want to.'

'Is it like a pact?'

'If you like.'

He had to believe in the other voice, it was all he had. But he couldn't help seeing someone outside hurriedly pulling it by the arm – bars, cinemas, rendezvous, street corners – and plunging together into that dizzy whirl of animated faces, odd words here and there, stray ones maybe, but always alluring, crafty, pushing him – him, her, the other voice – further and further away from himself. One day it would be forever and all I have to cling to is my own dark interior. On that other day there will be nothing around me, except the bars. He wanted to alert him to the necessity of their resisting together on that fragile bridge. Until some sunny day, if you'll wait for me outside.

Suddenly now, as it had before when he sensed that the phone would ring, something began to writhe inside him, announcing the voice's departure. He wanted to keep the other voice there awhile, with some story or other. The Chinese, he remembered, the Chinese shouted out lies about the quality of the harvest in order to deceive and drive away the evil gods. But he never thought that he had the right to lure the other voice into the darkness where he was lying. He understood more clearly now that it moved away when he tried in vain to reconstruct the face to which the other voice belonged. He thrashed about in the lake, sinking deeper every time he tried to get back up to the surface. The face came close and then moved away, cut off from him by the sinuous movement of the fish which made its outline shiver like the waves until, for a moment, it too seemed to be made of water. A blind man, he was guided by the voice. He wanted to shout for help, but the water poured into his mouth. He swallowed the forbidden words, they tasted of dry seaweed.

Before it hung up, the other voice just had time to say, 'I'll phone again tomorrow.'

He slowly ran his fingers over the silent phone. It was cold. There were no vibrant sounds escaping from the holes in the receiver; warming the room and filling it with colour. Everything else, the whole world that lived inside him, left with the other voice. That was the most difficult moment, between being deserted by the voice and waiting for them: Ana and Carlos. It wasn't a long moment. It got dark early on those first winter nights. He could see the darkness slowly spreading over the wall opposite the open window, so slowly that maybe, with his hands on the bars, he could frighten it away with a shout.

But he knew that the dark, unlike the Chinese gods, isn't afraid of shouts. It can't be deceived either.

Rather than sliding his back down the wall, just like every day, until he was sitting on the floor with his arms around his legs, and later gently rocking to and fro, to and fro, he decided instead to walk over to the window. A bell tolled in the distance, at nearly six in the afternoon. He clenched his teeth and went back inside, ready to face them when the night brought them back once more. He closed his eyes. As he waited, against the infinite background of his eyelids, with a great effort, he managed to make out more and more clearly, amongst shapes and spectres, something like the open fingers of a hand stretched out towards him.

Don't desert me, he begged inside, deep down, far off, upwards, outwards, in all directions. And he bent his head like someone praying. So that the hand could touch him, finally heralding the light. Some kind of light, even inside the darkness. Perhaps like that light which inhabited the other voice, so alive and ever more remote. Every day, at about five-fifteen in the afternoon. Because he wanted – and he wanted it for the sake of wanting – the light of the other voice, not their darkness, he made that choice.

XII

Little Monster

1

That summer, when Mother told me that cousin Alex was coming to spend the weekend with us at our rented house on the beach, I didn't like it one bit. Not because of him, I couldn't really remember what he looked like, it could have been any other of my cousins, aunts, uncles or grandparents. It was more because of myself, I'd just started growing in all directions, in a crazy kind of way. Legs and arms everywhere, hairs in the wrong places, my voice was breaking and it made me sound like a croaky duck, I wanted to hide from everyone. I'd only go out at dusk when the domestics – the *skivvies*, Father called them – were coming back from the beach. Then I'd walk for miles down by the sea, roll in the sand and sometimes cry and say over and over, little monster, little monster, nobody loves you. I couldn't stand anyone near me. A Mother insisting all the time that you should go to the beach the same time as *normal* people and a Father who looks at you as if you were the most disgusting creature on earth and just thinks of sticking you in the barracks so you'll learn what's good for you – that's punishment enough for one summer. As if my misfortunes weren't enough already now I was going to have to share *my* room with dear old cousin Alex. And I didn't want anyone to hear my croaky duck's voice or see my arms that were too long, my ostrich legs, my hairs in the wrong places.

I made a face, but Mother didn't pay any attention. She said that he was coming and soon, that he'd been studying hard the whole year, he'd passed the entrance exams for something or other and needed to rest and she had that obligation to Aunt Dulcinha, poor thing, so lonely, and apart from anything else Alex was a good boy, so studious, poor lad. That I hated more than anything; those good boys who were so studious and bespectacled, always going out with their duffel bags at lunchtime to buy beers and coca-colas and cigarettes for everyone, helping with the dishes and putting out those bloody annoying baskets on the green mat at the end of the table. I gave the Argentinian peach preserve a shove, the syrup spilled onto the table-cloth and I scowled. That was my way of saying, I don't need to see what he looks like to know for sure he's a wimp.

Just as I was dropping off to sleep later that same night when Mother told me Alex was coming, I tried to remember what he looked like and couldn't. In fact, I hadn't been able to remember what anyone looked like for the last two years, since I'd started to be a bit of a monster and my relatives nudged each other when I was around, sniggered and whispered things, looking slyly at me. I couldn't stand them, they thought they knew everything about me. They knew nothing, they knew bugger all about the enormous hatred I had for every single one of them, those gut-buckets, those sweaty chests with their feet covered in corns. I was never going to be like them, I'd always be different from everyone – the little monster. That was just how I was going to behave with cousin Alex, I decided; more and more the little monster until he couldn't stand it a minute longer and shoved off for good. I stood there staring hard at the bare mattress next to mine where he was going to sleep, until I filled the mattress with all my hatred so that he'd feel awful and leave the same day.

2

The day he was coming, and I knew because Mother wouldn't talk about anything else, she put clean sheets on the bed next to mine, told me to tidy up my comic books and put the clothes on the back of the chair away in the wardrobe. I went out a bit earlier and spent *ages* walking along the beach. I liked to go as far as the lighthouse on the way to Cidreira, where there were some dunes and it was nice just to lie there on the sand looking at the endless sea. Sometimes a ship would go by, and I'd ask where's it going? Where's it going? Pretty stupid really, I wasn't thinking where, just asking, where's it going, without thinking of the name or anything. Then I'd think as well what if I went straight out from here and into the sea and if I could walk on the water just like Jesus Christ and go straight ahead forever without stopping, where would I end up? I reckoned I'd end up in Africa, India, I dunno. I'd end up somewhere. Far away from there, from Tramandaí. Then a really round full moon started to rise up out of the sea and first I'd try and see Saint George and the dragon in it, then it occurred to me that was just stupid kids' stuff, and I thought of craters, deserts, and I could almost see them, the Sea of Tranquillity. Or was it Fertility? I looked and looked at it all, pottering around, until suddenly it was pitch black, and I had to go back to that bloody house with them, Father and Mother. On top of it all, on the way back I started to remember, feeling more and more pissed off, and because of that I walked even more slowly and it got darker and darker, now there'd be dear old cousin Alex there, he'd have wormed his way into *my* room.

A few yobs came along with a guitar and a bottle of Cinzano, arm in arm, singing some song or other. I veered away from them and paddled in the seawater, with my head down so they wouldn't bother me. From time to time I'd look back and all I'd hear was those yobbish voices further and further away, singing, *it's-so-dark-tonight/it's-the-moon's-night-off-tonight/ and-I'm-feeling-so-blue/'cos-I'm-here-without-you*. Idiots, I thought, because it wasn't the moon's night off at all, that'd be a new moon, not that huge great round, yellow moon, right there above the sea and above our heads. When I'd walked northwards for a bit and the yobs had disappeared, looking over my right shoulder I thought maybe now, if I go straight out from here I'll end up right over there in the very south of Africa, the Cape of Storms. Or was it the Cape of Good Hope? Then suddenly a whopping great shooting star came whizzing down, almost the same size as the moon, so big that I even stopped to see if I could hear the pssshhhhhhhhhh of the star falling into the sea. Nothing happened, so I said out loud, imitating that thin reedy voice of Dona Irineide, the Geography teacher, me-te-ors, what the great unwashed call shooting stars are really me-te-ors. I felt very learned and everything but it felt a bit flat, then I remembered you could make a wish, or three, I don't know. So I picked one and wished. That since cousin Alex had to be in that bloody house – and I couldn't possibly ask for him not to come, because he already had – at least he'd be OK and wouldn't be a pain.

Walking ever so slowly I amused myself like this along the way. Then I was so late that when I got home they'd already started to a make a fuss. Father was in his pyjamas and slippers, called me wicked and said he was going to forbid me to go to the beach at this unearthly hour and I replied that if he forbade me to go at that time then I'd stay locked in my room and I wouldn't *ever* go out again at any time, and Mother whispered, but I heard her, it's his age don't take any notice, don't pick on the lad, dear, and gave me some half-cold supper with sweet corn and I'd just opened my mouth to say that I wasn't a horse when she said that cousin Alex had arrived and was asleep, he was dead beat after the journey. She didn't need to say anything; sitting at the end of the table I'd already seen that chequered cowboy shirt hanging on the back of a chair. Even if I hadn't seen anything, I could sniff a smell in the air. Neither a nice nor a horrible smell, just the smell of a stranger who'd recently arrived after a journey. Dust, B.O., I dunno. I could hardly eat I was so full of hatred. Father went sourly off to bed, saying I'd see what was what in the barracks. Mother started playing about with the radio but all she got was interference between some stations in Spanish, *station L-R-One station L-R-Two*. No Elvis, who I liked and she pretended she didn't, just Gardel who she liked and I definitely didn't. I said I was going to bed too, Mother put her hand on my shoulder and ever so seriously asked me to promise I'd be polite to cousin Alex, poor thing his father had died and it was such a lot for Auntie Dulcinha to cope with and all that. I actually promised, it didn't cost anything. But I sat there twiddling my thumbs, praying that she wouldn't say that he was a good boy again, so studious, poor lad, otherwise my hatred would all come back. In the end she did, just when Gardel was singing *you knew the world wasn't big enough for all the humble joy in my poor heart*, and I went to bed full of hatred. For her, Father, cousin Alex, Auntie Dulcinha, the yobs on the beach, Gardel, everything.

3

I got the sand off my feet in the bidet, washed my face and stood in front of the mirror. Little monster, I said. More than once, three, twelve, twenty times I said it over and over again, looking at myself in the mirror before I went to bed, little, little monster, nobody, nobody loves you. I had a pee, brushed my teeth and gargled. It made me want to be sick, it always did. But I wasn't sick, I never was. I felt like curling up right there under the sink, like some mutt that's been chased off, and sleep there until the next morning so that they'd all see how miserable I was. My room wasn't just mine any more, I couldn't stay up late reading or anything, with the light on into the early hours because blasted cousin Alex was there and I'd promised to be polite to him, poor boy.

That room that was now no longer mine but mine and dear old cousin Alex's was at the back of the wooden house in a kind of extension next to a bathroom that before he arrived was just mine too but was now mine and his, how sickening. I put the light out, stood at the bathroom door and hung about there for a bit, standing in the darkened corridor before going in. I had to be ready to face that wall of specs, because – I knew his sort all right – he was bound to have left his greasy specs on *my* bedside table and those disgusting shiny black school shoes with the socks all stiff sticking out of the top and a stink of sweaty feet in the air, with him sprawled across the bed, snoring and farting like a pig. What hatred, what hatred I felt, standing there on that dark landing between the bathroom and the bedroom which weren't mine any more.

I opened the door ever so slowly. The sash window was raised, the light was turned off. There wasn't any stink in the air. The moonlight coming in through the window was so bright that I made my way through the dark to my bed without having to put my hand out or anything. I sat down, reached over to the bedside table and felt – no specs. Just my *Tarzan, the Invincible* book, from the Land-Sea-and-Air series. That was something at least, I thought, the creep doesn't wear glasses. I kept my pants and vest on, and lay down. There wasn't any sound of snoring, or any smell of fart in the air, just that rather heady perfume from the jasmine tree in the yard next door. My eyes were getting more used to the dark and I started to look over at the bed where cousin Alex was lying on the other side of the room.

The moonlight was shining right on him. He was lying on top of the sheets stark naked. My eyes were getting more and more used to the dark, and I could see Alex turned over on his right side, both hands closed together between his slightly bent legs. He seemed very big, he had to draw up his legs a bit, otherwise his feet would hit the end of the camp bed. He had a lot of hairs all over his body and the way the moonlight shone on them made the tip of each hair sparkle. His face was turned sideways, I couldn't see it. I could see those hairs sparkling – hairs in the right places, not in the wrong places, like mine – going down from his neck, across his chest and tummy, hidden and thicker just between where his hands were, then spread over his legs, down to his feet. Cousin Alex's curled up feet were very white, his father had died, he'd been studying the whole year and had passed the entrance exam for something or other I remembered. And he didn't make any sound when he was asleep, poor lad.

I lay there on my bed looking at him. After a while I began to hear him breathing and started to pay attention to my own breathing, until I got it the same as his. I was breathing, he was breathing. I folded my hands on my chest and rested my head against the head of the bed so I could see better. He'd folded his hands between his legs to sleep better, no doubt, poor lad, he was dead beat after the journey. I lay there looking at him, breathing slowly, at the same speed. Nice and slowly, so as not to wake him. I don't know why, but suddenly all my hatred went away. Lying there, watching cousin Alex asleep stark naked beneath that huge moon, the heady smell of the jasmines coming in through the open window, made me feel something, I couldn't really tell whether it was dizziness, sleepiness, disgust or maybe that hatred ever so slowly changing into something else, quite what I didn't yet know.

4

In the morning I stayed in bed until almost midday. I heard some sounds of people waking up but I didn't move or look around, just stayed with my face turned towards the wall.

Then there were some other sounds, the toilet flushing, a tap being turned on, a spoon knocking against a cup in the kitchen, Mother's voice saying that was just like me, sleeping until my bottom took root and a deeper voice that wasn't Father's, saying something I couldn't hear. Then the sound of doors shutting, and silence. I knew they'd all gone to the beach, and I thought about getting up to poke around a bit in cousin Alex's things, no one would see. But I began to sink into that thing I called *half-sleep*, because it wasn't quite sleep. My prick got so stiff every morning that it would hurt, so I'd press it against the sheet, there seemed to be something inside it that was going to explode but it didn't, I started to feel all hot inside and out while I thought of filthy kinds of things: one of black Dina's breasts that I saw once by the pond, people moaning and the bed creaking in Father and Mother's room. I hardly knew anything about these things. But they were what I always thought of in that half-sleep, my prick pressed against the mattress, until everything got more sleepy than half-sleepy. Then I'd fall deep into the well and not remember anything else.

I only got out of bed when Mother knocked on the door and said that lunch was nearly on the table. I looked at cousin Alex's bed, all unmade and thought the stupid idiot must be sitting down there in the living room as if the house was his, drinking beer with Father. I slipped on my shorts, washed my face in the bathroom and hung about as much as I could, so I didn't have to see anyone or anyone see me. But when I came out and went through the house, there was only Mother pottering about in the kitchen and Father sitting on the verandah step, reading *The People's Post*. I looked around, there wasn't any sign of cousin Alex apart from the chequered cowboy shirt from the night before there on the back of the chair. I didn't ask anything, just sat at the end of the table, scratching the tablecloth with the tip of my fork. Until Mother said,

'Alex just loved the beach. The poor boy hadn't ever seen the sea before. You should have seen him, he was just like a child. He stayed there, there's no way he'd come back.'

Well done, I thought, he'll go as red as a lobster. And tonight he'll have to rub talcum powder on his back and toothpaste on his nose and turn over and over in bed unable to sleep, because when you're sunburnt like that even the sheets hurt your skin. He'll moan and get on my wick all night and tomorrow or the next day he'll start peeling like a snake changing its skin until he gets all sunburnt again and his skin goes tough like leather and he starts feeling ace, in his moccasins, white trousers and red Banlon shirt, all sunburnt and stupid stupid stupid. I was thinking about all this while Mother served up the food and Father didn't even look straight at me, but just read his paper, shook his head and said dreadful-absolutely-dreadful and I couldn't eat properly or feel much hatred. Thinking those things was more a way of exercising my badness, I had to practise every day so I didn't forget how to be a little monster. I drank almost a litre of gooseberry cordial, pure sugar, felt sick in the pit of my stomach and pushed the plate away without any appetite. I said I wasn't feeling very well, and Father said no wonder, little Lord Muck sleeping like a convict, you'll get TB, Mother said leave the kid alone, don't pick on him like that, he said that's why I was so cocky because she was like a slave to me, she said she'd rented that house by the beach to see if she could relax a bit, not so that he could make her life even more hellish, it was torture as it was – and they both started shouting louder and louder while I took the opportunity to dive off to my room without anyone seeing me.

The bedroom turned into an oven after lunch. The sun beat down on the zinc roof and it got boiling hot in there. I thought that if I stayed in there all that damned cordial would start boiling away in my stomach until a red slimy foam poured out of my mouth and all over the floor, knocking me against the walls. At least then maybe someone in the world would pay me some attention. I picked up the Tarzan book, went through the kitchen where they were still bellowing at each other, and lay down in the hammock under the cinnamon trees where a breeze was blowing. But even there, in that nice shade, I couldn't stop thinking how my life was hell. And if one day I started walking straight out across the sea, even if I couldn't walk on the buggering water like Jesus Christ, it'd be great for everyone if I just went under and no one could find me ever again drowned forever at the bottom of the sea like the Titanic. I tried to read but those priests rabbiting on in the caves of Opar were getting on my nerves a bit.

5

A brown face with black hair was peering over the top of the hammock at me. A brown face very close to mine, smelling strongly of sweat and seawater. I almost shouted, because as soon as I opened my eyes and met with that face and that smell I didn't remember that I'd lain down in the hammock after lunch. I think I was dreaming of Jad-bal-ja, the golden lion and that was what I thought of when I saw that brown face peering at me over the top of the hammock. But all brown, gypsyish, it wasn't a lion's face, it was cousin Alex's, with thick black eyebrows stuck over his nose. He smiled at me but his face was too close, I couldn't smile back or anything, however polite that might have been. I looked down at the Tarzan book on my lap, then I frowned to see whether he'd go. But he wouldn't it seemed. He pushed the hammock, backed off a little and stood there watching me swinging like an idiot and him watching me with his arms folded, legs apart:

'Auntie said there's a shower out here', he said with a slightly hoarse voice, deeper than Father's, and very well-spoken. 'So I can get rid of this sand before I go inside. Where is it?'

'Over there', I pointed to the back of the house. He looked at me a bit longer with his arms folded. I could only see his face and his hair stiff with salt and sand and parts of his body going up and down with the swinging of the hammock, his legs apart. At least he doesn't wear boxer trunks, I thought, those baggy nylon trunks that you can see just by looking at someone who wears them that they've never been to the beach in their life, yokel trunks. But his were black, quite decent actually:

'Don't you like going to the beach?' he asked. 'Auntie said so.'

'No', I said. I knew it: Mother had said I didn't like going to the beach; that I didn't talk to anyone; that I slept until lunchtime; that I stayed locked in my room; that I kicked the door and everything, she must have told him everything – that I was a monster. Then I thought it wasn't his fault, poor boy, it was her going on and on at him and I tried to be more polite: 'I only like to at dusk, when the sun's going down.'

'Oh', he said. And I thought it was brilliant that he didn't say anything else, like I should get up earlier, take advantage of the sun and all that rubbish. I couldn't quite see him properly, so I stretched out a leg, stuck my toes in the grass and made the hammock stop swinging. Then I looked. He smiled again with white, white teeth; either that or they just seemed very white because he was incredibly brown. He hadn't got a bit red from the sun. He brushed his hands over his chest, tummy and legs and the sand fell off onto the ground. Mother's voice shouted from inside for him to come and have lunch. I opened the book, made as if I was going to start reading and he smiled again and slowly walked over to the shower. He's like a lion, really brown, I thought, walking like that, kind of sauntering. And I started to read.

His muscular, steel-like fingers grasped one of the bars in the middle. Standing turned away from me under the shower, his back was straight, broad, with a little triangle of curly black hair, wider up towards his waist and narrower down towards his bottom. He turned on the shower and shouted out when the freezing cold water began to pour out. *With his left hand he grabbed his other one and, leaning one of his knees against the door, slowly bent his right elbow.* Each of his arms was almost as thick as my thigh. The water began to wash away the sand and I could see his body properly now that it was no longer hidden. I couldn't stop staring. *Rippling like molten steel, the muscles of his forearm and his biceps grew until the bar gradually bent towards him.* He turned around, pulled his trunks away from him with both hands and moved his body forward a bit so the water would hit his stomach and go down inside them. He slipped his hands inside his trunks, then looked at me through the drops from the shower and turned his head, spitting out water. *The ape-man smiled as he grabbed the iron bar again.* When he turned off the shower and shook his wet hair, the drops spattered my face and Mother called him again from inside. Suddenly and without meaning to, I slammed the book shut, leapt out of the hammock and ran off towards the front door.

6

For the rest of that day I couldn't do anything else. It's almost as if on the other days I did do something else, apart from messing around here and there, boiling hot, sleeping or wandering about on the beach. Well I couldn't even do that. My heart suddenly started beating wildly, as if I'd had a fright, but not exactly, because I wasn't afraid of anything. Or perhaps I was; afraid of something faceless and nameless, because it wasn't coming from outside but from within me. A cold chill, even under the blistering heat of the sun, looking at my flattened shadow like a green Martian monster and a hot shiver, even behind the house where there were actually slugs it was so damp. All I knew was that for all the world I didn't want to be anywhere near cousin Alex.

From where I was hiding, I saw him go into the bedroom and pull down the blinds on the window because he must have been going to have an afternoon nap. *Everyone* in the whole world took an afternoon nap, except me, the little monster. I followed with the tip of my finger a silvery slug trail in that cool place behind the house. Time passed. When I came out into the sun again I saw that it was much later because my shadow was no longer so flat or monstrous. Then, ever so slowly, I went right up to the bedroom window and without making a sound pushed up the blind; gently, as if it was a gust of wind. He was naked, with his back to the window. Just below that triangle of curly black hair at his waist, his trunks had left a white mark which seemed even whiter now that the red from the sun was beginning to burn. He was lying propped up on his left arm. His right arm, which I could only half see, was bent at the waist and disappeared in front of his body. And it was moving. Lying quite still cousin Alex was just moving the right arm which I couldn't see completely because he had his back to me. Faster and faster, I held my breath, my chin resting on the window, and faster and faster, until he moaned, first softly, then louder, sighed, his whole body shaking, turned face down on the bed and buried his face in the pillow. From the tips of his fingers, which were almost touching the floor, ran a whitish, silvery slime which left a trail on the floor just like that of the slugs at the back of the house.

It was still very early but I went for a walk on the beach. I ran out across the sand towards the lighthouse and when I saw there was no one else around I started to shout out, Sumatra Tantor Zanzibar Bukula Mensahib Nikima Jad-bal-ja. That sort of thing, just like music. You could sing it and I did.

Every time one of my feet hit the sand I'd shout Sumatra or Bukula or Nikima, as if I'd just escaped from a loony bin. I couldn't help myself. I only stopped when my heart was pounding too much and my face was bathed in sweat, right in front of the lighthouse. Then I looked around, saw there was no one there, and did something I'd *never* done before. I took off my shorts and shirt, threw them down on the sand and waded into the water stark naked.

I spread my legs and arms and threw myself right into the foam. I hit my bum on the sand on the sea bed but it didn't hurt. Then I turned over on my front and started rubbing my rock-hard prick on the nice soft wet sand. It got harder and harder, there seemed to be something trying to get out, a glistening silvery strand. But nothing came out, the sand was burning, the salt was stinging. Then I went and pulled my arse apart with both hands right where the waves were breaking, and stayed like that, letting the waves break and the warm foam from the late afternoon wash into my open arse. It made me feel dizzy, I couldn't help thinking of cousin Alex's right arm going faster and faster as if something was going to explode. Nothing did explode, I dug my nails into my arm, said fifteen times little-monster-little-monster-nobody-loves-you and didn't know what else to do about my life, about that fear or whatever it was that wanted to get out, had to get out of me but couldn't work out how.

My heart was pounding away when I got home. Mother was laying the table for dinner. Go and wash your hands, Father said without looking at me, he never looked at me. I let the water run without looking at myself in the mirror. When I came back cousin Alex was sitting there, scratching the chequered tablecloth with the serrated edge of his knife. I didn't look at him, but even without looking I could see that he'd put on a pale white Banlon shirt and combed his hair. I didn't want to look at him. But then Mother put the eggs and steak on my plate and Father said don't stick your nose in your plate like that, child, blimey, you're just like a savage. It made me go red with embarrassment him talking to me like that in front of cousin Alex and I couldn't help raising my head and looking up. He twitched those black eyebrows of his and winked at me. As if we had a secret. I sat there like an idiot looking at him on and off. He kept on looking at me over the jug of cordial (orange at dinner, not gooseberry). From time to time he'd wink, then he'd smile, without anyone seeing. As if there was something going on just between him and me. Something that had to do with that desire of mine to keep staring and staring at him? It might have been that desire, mixed with that fear, that arm of his moving faster and faster, that silvery strand of shiny slime trailing along the floor; like the syrup from the peach preserve that I spilled on the table cloth again but, before Father could call me a pig, Mother asked,

'Wouldn't you like to ask Alex out for a walk around the square and have a beer in town?'

The three of them sat there looking at me. I rubbed my finger in the syrup from the peach preserve and licked it slowly as I looked at cousin Alex and invited him,

'Shall we?'

He stared back. And said yes.

7

Blue, but they weren't exactly blue. I only saw that halfway through my first beer. Dark blue that faded gradually, kind of bleached where his body rubbed them. On the knees, on the bum, at the front where they rubbed against the lump of his prick, behind the fly. They had a zipper fly just like a woman's skirt, instead of buttons like mine. I'd seen some like that before, but only in films about teenagers and just a few on some trendy blokes down on the beach. It gave you a certain look. A nice look, a modern look. I'd hardly said a word, but after that sip of beer I got up courage and said,

'Your jeans are brilliant.'

'They're Lee', he said. 'American, imported.'

'Where d'you buy them?'

'Only on the black market. Do you want me to get you some?'

I asked if it was difficult, he said there were ways, he had a contact in Porto. Then he said they weren't as nice brand new, but you could fade them with bleach in the washtub. Better to let them just fade on their own, except it took a while. I asked if his were bleached or if he'd let them fade on their own. He wasn't paying attention and didn't hear. He took his packet of Ministers out of his pocket and asked if I wanted one. I said no, if Father knew. He lit one and blew the smoke up in the air, raising his head a bit. Again I thought of the golden lion. I reckon I was getting a bit drunk with all that beer because I suddenly couldn't stop staring at cousin Alex sitting there next to me at the table in the pavement cafe. He looked huge, he looked brilliant, he looked handsome. Without making any effort to look anything, he wasn't a show-off. I don't think he really knew what he was like. He was sitting there next to me as if he was some ordinary bloke, smoking, drinking beer and smiling at me occasionally. I thought that everyone going past and sitting at the other tables was staring at him and thinking who can that kid be. Suddenly I felt kind of proud of all those people seeing me there next to him and something weird happened. For a second, I stopped feeling like a monster.

I looked at my arm on the table. My rather thin, suntanned arm. But it looked nice too. I looked at my brown hand, with hardly any hairs on it, then I touched my hair with it and thought I could let it grow a bit, just like cousin Alex's. And when I touched my hair with my hand like that, I noticed my back was really bent forward, as if I was trying to protect from the world something hidden deep in my chest. So I forced my shoulders back, and didn't feel at all like a monster when I looked at cousin Alex again and saw the full moon rising behind his head and behind the roof of Willy's Tavern.

The waiter called him *sir* when he asked whether he wanted another beer. He had a way of knowing how to sit in a bar, the way I'd have one day. He asked whether I wanted one too, I said I did, despite being a bit drunk. He filled my glass to the brim. As I wiped my finger over the head, he said,

'Auntie told me she's worried about you.' I thought bloody hell, she's been filling his head with stuff again, now he's going to start giving me his opinion and advice and everything. But he didn't let me say anything, he just said, 'She says she thinks you're really lonely. That you haven't got any friends.'

That was all it needed. When he said that – Shazam! Only in reverse, instead of making the bloke brilliant, it made him even more of a wimp. I started to feel like a monster again. Poor poor poor me, I thought, my eyes filled with tears of self-pity, poor wounded me. I felt a bit sick from all that beer and felt like getting up and saying I was going home. Then cousin Alex said,

'I told her it's your age. That it'll pass. That I was just like you, a bit shy. But it'll pass, you'll see it'll pass.' I nearly said I was sure that with me it would never pass. That I was going to stay like that forever to the end of the world a little, little horrible monster, different from everyone else, with everyone laughing quietly and saying things when I went past. But he said,

'I'm your friend.'

I stopped feeling like a monster again. No one had ever said that to me before. It was then that things started to happen very quickly, I felt like laughing, I started talking and couldn't stop, he started talking and talking as well about his Medical degree, everything he was going to study, things to do with people's minds, with long words, psycho something or other, about books by blokes with long names as well, about records, films, and he said he'd give me some things to read and listen to that I'd like, and I thought it wouldn't happen because I'd be stuck the whole year in that wilderness of Passo da Guanxuma and him in Porto Alegre and then it'd get difficult, until we didn't see each other again and I started feeling sad, then he told me Mother had said that she'd been thinking about sending me to study in Porto Alegre and at first I thought I was going to really shit myself, then I gradually got my courage up and my heart felt happy, it was going to be just like in a film, going on the tram on my own into town to that Parthenon place where he said he lived and I'd go there every Sunday evening, I'd stay in his room listening on the Dansette to those records he said he was going to show me, me with my Lee jeans just like his, first faded from bleach and then faded on their own, from the sun and rain and everyone would look when we went into the cinema together and they'd whisper in a different way because I wasn't a monster any more, just because we looked great together, that was why they'd talk and point, me and cousin Alex walking in the evening through some square or along some pavement right in that place I'd never been called Parthenon, and Parthenon was almost as nice and far away as Sumatra, Zanzibar, Uganda and I got up courage and told him I wanted to be a musician and play rock and roll just like Elvis, that I knew some bits of songs by heart in English and he sang laughing *it's now or never*, just a bit, then he stroked my hair and said I'd have to grow a kiss-curl so that it fell down over my forehead when I went *yeah* wiggling my hips, and just for a laugh I went *yeah yeah yeah*, and he killed himself laughing and I killed myself laughing too, and he ordered another beer and I lit a cigarette and coughed and coughed and he patted me on the back, the people around us were staring and he started to tell me how after he'd qualified he was going to travel a lot by ship around the whole world and I asked if he'd go to Zanzibar as well and he killed himself laughing again and said yes, did I want to go with him to Zanzibar, sure I said and I started imagining it all as he told me; he was going to be a great doctor, one of those modern ones who cure other people's minds so that everyone will be happy all the time forever without any guilt, he said, he was so nice, everyone around was staring, I was laughing, he was laughing and we were getting more and more drunk until I tried to get up to go to the toilet and almost fell over the table. Then he took hold of me by the arm and couldn't stop laughing as he told me it was time to go otherwise Father and Mother would go crazy.

8

We only stopped laughing on the way from the front door to the bedroom, so that Father and Mother wouldn't wake up. Gone midnight, Alex saw on his wrist watch. I shut the door, threw myself on the bed and carried on laughing. We'd look at each other from time to time and laugh even more. For ages like that, like a couple of nutcases. My stomach was hurting from laughing so much, I said I was going to the bathroom for a pee and I'd be right back. I took a while, it was like I'd drunk gallons. When I got back, he'd taken all his clothes off and was lying on his back on the bed. You'll catch a cold, I thought of saying. I just thought of saying it, then I saw it wasn't draughty or anything. And I went over to my bed as I looked at his Lee jeans, his Banlon shirt, his moccasins and his pants chucked on the floor, not really knowing what to do with the window open, the full moon and cousin Alex starkers on the bed next to me. I tried not to look at him. But he was looking straight at me when he said oddly, as if he meant something other than what he was saying,

'It's really hot, don't you reckon?'

'Yeah', I said. And then I couldn't stop staring at him. I got a bit cheeky and really stared, because I felt like it and it was nice staring. I ran my eyes down his chest, following those hairs that got thicker up there, just under his neck, around his pink nipples, then got narrower as they went down his stomach and turned into a kind of curly little strand, until they started to get curlier and thicker again, between his legs. He had his hand between his legs, just where the hair was most curly:

'I spied on you sleeping this afternoon', I told him.

'I saw you', he said. 'I wasn't asleep, I was having a wank.'

I went bright red. I looked over to the Tarzan the Invincible book on the bedside table. On top of a tree, Tarzan was aiming an arrow at a *bwana* talking to two pygmy negroes in front of a hut. What if he shoots the arrow? I thought:

'Have you ever shot your load?' he asked.

'No', I said. 'Never. I don't even know how you do it.'

'Do you want me to teach you?' He was smiling again. That golden lion's head of his, with his white, white teeth:

'Yeah', I said.

He took his hand out from between his legs, patted the bed beside him and called me over,

'Sit here, I'll show you how. Get your clothes off and sit beside me.'

I took them off and threw them on the floor, on top of his clothes. Then I sat down on his bed, just in my pants. Horrible pants, all baggy, not like his. He was sweating a bit. The smell of sweat was mixed with the smell of a perfume that I think was aftershave, plus the smell of the jasmine bush coming in through the open window. I could hear the boom-boom of my heart in my chest. He was ever so close to me. I crossed my legs, with my back to him, facing the window:

'Turn round this way', he said.

He stretched out his hand and touched my knee. I gradually

turned round until I was facing him. He sat down on the bed, faced me and crossed his legs too. He rested one of his hands on my thigh, then moved it up and slowly pulled down my pants. I stretched out my leg so that he could pull them off and throw them on the floor, on top of our clothes. Now I was completely naked, my prick as stiff as his, I'd seen it. He wasn't hiding it, it wasn't ugly. I almost got embarrassed, but he fixed his eyes right on mine, without smiling or blinking. He brought his right hand over to his stiff prick, while with his left he took hold of my right hand and moved it over to my stiff prick. He held on to my arm, slowly guiding it so that I'd move it up and down, just like he was doing. He was so handsome. He squirmed and groaned a bit. I shut my eyes. If I walk straight out from here straight on I'll end up in Africa, I thought like an idiot. The thing that wanted to explode was rising up inside again. I opened my legs wider and threw my body forward. He got closer. Then he took hold of my arm again, spat on the palm of my hand and moved it over to his prick. He spat on the palm of his hand and moved it over to my prick. Warm moist firm soft. The bed creaked. I got even closer. That thing was growing inside me like a madman in a straitjacket, as if my body was going to explode and out of it would shoot balloons, little coloured flags for St. Anthony's day, gold Christmas tree decorations, confetti and Carnival streamers, who knows what else. Faster, he said. Faster, let's come together. The two of us seemed to be alone in a boat drifting on the sea in the middle of a storm. Sumatra Tantor Bukula Nikima, I was going to shout out loud, when that thing started to gather inside me like a wave building up a long way from the beach while we waited for it to arrive here on the shore, not caring a bit if Father and Mother could hear and the whole neighbourhood and the whole town woke up. He got even closer. I pressed my chest up against his. He buried his mouth in mine as I felt the palm of my hand gradually getting wet from that strand of shiny silver which was coming out of him and I knew that a shiny wet silver strand was coming out of me too just like the one coming out of him.

Come with me, he called. And I came.

He ran his moist hands over my back. I ran my moist hands over his back. He took his mouth away from mine, then rested his head on my shoulder. My heart was pounding away, he could hear it. Our sweat mingled. His heart was pounding away, I heard it when I rested my head on his shoulder. I kept on running my hands over his back. They were all sticky with the silvery water that he'd taught me to draw out from inside. He didn't mind getting sticky from my water. I didn't mind getting sticky from his water either. I didn't feel a bit disgusted. He ran his tongue over the curve in my neck. I tangled my fingers in that triangle of curly hair at his waist. I don't know how long it lasted. I know that suddenly we separated and, looking at each other, started laughing like crazy again.

9

Very early the next morning we went to the beach together. He taught me to dive and float, I pointed to the horizon and showed him the way to Africa, the Indies. After lunch, in the boiling oven of the bedroom with the zinc roof, he showed me the way to other places. When it was time for him to go, in the evening, I helped him pack his clothes. But I didn't go to the bus station. I watched, hidden, from the corner. Then I ran along the pavement behind the bus, until he looked out of the window and shouted something that I couldn't quite make out. It sounded like Zanzibar, Parthenon, something like that. He kept on waving until the bus rounded the bend, in the red dust of the road to Osório.

That night I tried to find some music on the radio. No Gardel or Elvis. Instead I found Maísa, who Father said I wasn't old enough to listen to. Depraved she is, he said and I didn't know what that meant. At bedtime, Mother looked at me at said softly,

'You seem to be missing Alex an awful lot.'

I said I wasn't. And I wasn't lying. I knew that he'd stayed with me forever. She went to bed and I turned off the radio. Alone in the living room, in silence, I was no longer a monster. I sat there looking at my thin brown hand, with hardly any hairs on it. I knew that cousin Alex had stayed with me forever. Right there, in the palm of my hand.

XIII

Dragons...

'Because he sees with great clarity causes and effects, he completes the six steps at the right time and mounts toward heaven on them at the right time, as though on six dragons.'
('*Ch'ien*, The Creative': *I Ching, the Book of Changes*)

I've got a dragon living with me.
No, it's not true.
I haven't really got a dragon. And even if I did have, he wouldn't live with me or with anyone else. There's nothing harder for dragons to imagine than sharing their space, whether with another dragon or with some ordinary person like me. Or an unusual person, as I imagine others must be. They're solitary creatures, dragons. Almost as solitary as I felt when I was left alone in this flat after he went. I say *almost* because during all that time he was with me I nurtured the illusion that my isolation was over forever. And I say *illusion* because the other day, on one of those mornings barren with his absence, though fortunately it's getting less and less frequent (the barrenness, not his absence), I had this thought: *Men need the illusion of love in the same way that they need the illusion of God; the illusion of love so that they won't fall into that awful well of utter solitude; the illusion of God, so that they won't lose themselves in the chaos of disorder and anomie.*

It sounded grandiloquent and wise like an idea that wasn't mine, that's how stupid my thoughts tend to be. And I made a quick note of it on the napkin in the bar where I was sitting. I wrote down something else too but I spilt coffee over it. To this day I haven't been able to work out what it says. Or else I've avoided trying, afraid of my – fortunately undecipherable – lucidity on that day.

I'm getting confused, I'm drifting off all over the place.

The napkin, the sentence, the coffee stain, my fear – that'll have to come later. All these things I'm talking about now; the specialness of dragons, the ordinariness of people like me, I only discovered later. Slowly, as I tried to understand him in his absence. Understanding him less and less, attempting to make my understanding seductive enough to convince him to come back, and deeper and deeper so that this understanding might help me *to*. I can't say. When I'm thinking like this I make a list of propositions such as: *to* be a less ordinary person; *to* be stronger; more sure of myself, calmer, happier; *to* get by with the minimum of pain. All those things we decide to do or become when something we assumed to be great comes to an end, and there's nothing to be done but go on living.

So, let it be sweet. Every morning, when I open the windows to let in the sunshine or the greyness of a day, that's just what I repeat, let it be sweet. When it's sunny and the sun strikes my face creased with sleep or insomnia, as I watch the particles of dust floating in the air like a little universe, I repeat seven times for luck: let it be sweet let it be sweet let it be sweet and so on. But if someone asked me what had to be sweet maybe I wouldn't have an answer. *Everything* is so vague it might as well be nothing.

No one will ask anything, I think to myself. Then I carry on telling myself about it, as if I were both the old man telling the story and the child listening, sitting on my lap. That was the image which occurred to me this morning when, opening the window, I decided I couldn't bear to let another day go by without telling this story about dragons. I managed to avoid it until the middle of the afternoon. It hurts a little. Not a fresh wound any more, just a little rose thorn, or something of the sort that you try to dig out of the palm of your hand with the point of a needle. But if you don't manage to pluck it out, that little thorn might stop being a little pain and turn into a big sore.

That's how things are at the moment as I sit here. The sharp point of a needle balanced between the fingers of my right hand hovering over the open palm of my left hand. A few notes around me, made a long time ago, the paper napkin from the bar with those wise words that don't sound like mine and those other coffee-stained ones which I can't or don't want to or pretend I can't decipher.

I still haven't begun.

I really wish I could say *Once upon a time*. I still can't.

But I have to begin somehow. And I reckon that, after all, this way, not beginning properly, confused, drifting about, repetitively like this, is as good or bad as any other way of beginning a story. Above all if it's a story about dragons.

I enjoy saying *I've got a dragon living with me*, even though it's not true. As I was saying, a dragon never belongs to or lives with anyone. Whether it's an ordinary person like me or whether it's a unicorn, a salamander, a harpy, an elf, a wood nymph, a mermaid or an ogre. I doubt whether a dragon gets on better with those mythological beings that are more akin to his nature than he does with a human being. Not that they're unsociable. On the contrary, sometimes a dragon can be as kind and submissive as a geisha. It's just that their customs are different.

No one can really understand a dragon. They never show what they're feeling. Who could comprehend, for example, that as soon as they wake up (and this can happpen at any time, at three in the afternoon or eleven at night, since their day and night take place inside them, although it's more likely between seven and nine in the morning because that's the time for dragons) they always thrash their tails three times, as if they were in a rage, breathing fire through their nostrils and incinerating anything within a radius of over five metres? Today I wonder; perhaps that's their clumsy way of saying, as I tend to say these days, when they wake up – let it be sweet.

But at the time he was living with me, I tried to – let's say – adapt him to circumstances. I'd say please try to understand, darling, those common people on the next floor down have complained about your tail thrashing on the floor last night at four in the morning. The baby woke up, they said, he wouldn't let anyone sleep after that. Besides, when you wake up in the lounge, the plants get burnt up in the searing heat of your breath. And when you wake up in the bedroom, that pile of books on the bedside table turns to ashes.

He wouldn't promise to mend his ways. And I know very well how ridiculous this all sounds. A dragon never thinks he's wrong. In fact he never is. Everything he does that might seem dangerous, eccentric or in the slightest bit rude to a human being like me is just part of the strange nature of dragons. The following mornings, afternoons and nights, when he woke up again the neighbours would complain again and day by day the yellow primulas and the purple and green begonias and Kafka, Salinger, Pessoa, Lispector and Borges would get more and more scorched. Until just the two of us were left in that flat amongst the ashes. Ashes are like silk to a dragon, but never to a human because they remind us of destruction and death, not pleasure. They cross with impunity, with relish, over the threshold between two zones; one hidden, the other more worldly. Something we find hard to understand, or at least to accept.

Aside from anything else, I couldn't see him. Dragons are invisible you know. Did you know that? I didn't. It's so slow and difficult telling this story – has your patience run out yet? Of course, obviously you want to know how, after all, I was so sure of his existence if I claim I couldn't see him. If you were to say that he'd laugh. If, like men and hyenas, dragons possessed the dubious gift of laughter. You would think him perhaps ironic, but he would be quite unconcerned as he asked, but do you only believe in what you can see, then. If you said yes, he'd talk about unicorns, salamanders, harpies, wood nymphs, mermaids and ogres. Perhaps about fairies too or voodoo orishas. Or atoms, black holes, white dwarves, quasars and protozoa. And he'd say in that slightly pedantic tone, '*Anyone who only believes in what is visible has a very small world. There isn't room for dragons in those small worlds with walls that are inaccessible to what is not visible*'.

He really liked those words beginning with *in* – *invisible, inaccessible, incomprehensible* – which mean the opposite of what they should. He himself was quite the opposite of what he should be. So much so that when I thought he was being intractable, to use a word he'd like, I actually suspected him of being the opposite – oozing with affection. I sometimes thought of dealing with him like that, the wrong way round, so that we'd be happier together. I never dared. And now he's gone it's too late to attempt any refined harmonies.

He smelled of mint and rosemary. I believed in his existence because of that green smell of herbs crushed in the palms of both one's hands. There were other signs, other auguries. But I want to dwell on the smells for a moment before going on. Don't believe it if someone, even someone who doesn't have a small world, says that dragons smell of horses after a race, or of dogs from the streets after it's been raining. Of closed rooms, mould, rotten fruit, dead fish or the beach at low tide – that's never been the smell of dragons.

They smell of mint and rosemary. When he got in, the whole flat would be impregnated with that aroma. Even the neighbours, the ones from the next floor down, asked whether I was using incense or burning herbs to exorcise the flat. Everything all right, the wife asked. She had innocent blue eyes. Her husband didn't say anything, didn't even say hello. I reckon he thought it was one of those Indian herbs that people tend to smoke when they live in flats, listening to very loud music. The wife said the baby slept better when that smell started to drift down the stairs, more strongly in the evening, and that the baby smiled as if he were dreaming. Without saying a word, I knew that the baby must be dreaming of dragons, unicorns or salamanders, that was one way that his world could gradually become bigger. But babies usually forget those things when they stop being babies, although they possess the strange faculty of seeing dragons – something of which only more ample worlds are capable.

I learnt the trick of noticing when the dragon was next to me. Once, we went down in the lift together with that woman with the innocent-blue-eyes and her baby, who also had innocent-blue-eyes. The baby stared at me the whole time. Then it stretched out its hands to the left of me where the dragon was. Dragons always stand on your left, so they can talk straight to your heart. The air next to me became light and vaguely purplish. A sign that he was happy. Him, the dragon, and the baby too and me and the woman and the Japanese woman who got in on the sixth floor and a young man with a beard on the third. We smiled sweetly, a bit gormlessly, going down together in the lift on what I remember was an April afternoon – that's the month of dragons – in that atmosphere of fluid eternity that only dragons, but only sometimes, know how to convey.

I loved him for things like that. And I still love him, maybe even now, maybe even without quite knowing the exact meaning of that arid word – *love*. If not the whole time, then at least when I'm remembering moments like that. Which, unfortunately, is not often. Severity and contrariness seem to be more constant in the nature of dragons than levity and straightforwardness. But I wanted to talk about the time before the smell. There were other signs, I said earlier. Vague, all of them.

On the days leading up to his arrival I'd wake up in the middle of the night, my heart beating wildly. There'd be a cold sweat on the palms of my hands. Without knowing why, on the mornings afterwards I'd start to buy flowers, clean the house, go to the supermarket and the market to fill the flat with roses and palms and those nice plump strawberries and gleaming bunches of grapes and shiny aubergines (dragons, I found out later, love looking at aubergines) which I couldn't eat myself. I'd lay them out on dishes, in the corners, with flowers and candles and ribbons, so that the place would look nicer.

I felt a kind of hunger. But a hunger for seeing, not eating. I'd sit in the neat and tidy lounge, with the carpet brushed, the curtains washed, baskets of fruit, vases of flowers, I'd light a cigarette and sit there chewing over with my eyes the beauty of these clean ordered things, unable to eat anything with my mouth, just hungry for seeing. As the house became more lovely I became uglier and uglier, thinner and thinner, with heavy bags under my eyes and hollow cheeks. For I couldn't sleep or eat as I waited for him. Now, now I'm going to be happy I thought the whole time with a hysterical certainty. Until that smell of rosemary and mint began to get stronger and then, one day, slipped just like a breeze under the door and ever so slowly settled in the hallway, on the living-room sofa, in the bathroom, in my bed. He had arrived.

I only discovered those rhythms little by little. Even the smell of mint and rosemary, I only found out that was what it was when I came across some herbs on a market stall. My heart leapt, I imagined he was close by. I followed the smell until I was leaning over the stall and saw two green bunches, the mint with its tiny little leaves, the rosemary with its long stalks and leaves like thorns, but they didn't hurt. I asked what they were called, the man told me, and I didn't forget. With the sheer intoxication of it, on the following days I'd say again and again when the longing came over me, rosemary mint rosemary mint rosemary.

Before that, still earlier, my premonitions about his visit brought only anxiety, palpitations, nail-biting distress. It wasn't good. I couldn't work, go to the cinema or sink into any other of those mundane occupations which people like me occupy their lives with. All I could think about was pretty things for the house and getting myself nice to meet him. My anxiety was such that I became uglier as the days went by. And when he eventually did arrive, I'd never looked so ugly. Dragons don't forgive ugliness. Let alone ugliness in those whom they honour with their rare visits.

After he came, with the prettiness of the house contrasting with the ugliness of my body, everything gradually began to fall apart. Like pain, not happiness. Now now now I'm going to be happy, I kept on saying – now now now. And I strained to look in all the corners to see if I could find at least the reflections of his greenish-silver scales, a fleeting light, the arrow-shaped tip of his tail through the crack of an open door or the smoke from his nostrils which changed colour depending on his mood. Which was nearly always a bad one, and the smoke black. On those days I'd get crazier and crazier, wanting so urgently to be happy right now. Noticing my distress, he became more and more distant. He'd stay away, withdraw and pretend to leave. His smell of herbs became fainter and fainter until it was no more than a green hint in the air. I breathed deeper, getting breathless in my effort to see him, day after day, while the flowers and fruits rotted in the vases, baskets and corners, and those tiny little black flies buzzed ominously around them.

Everything was rotting away more and more without my noticing, so grief-stricken was I with the impossibility of having him. Concerned only with my pain; which was rotting too and smelling bad. Then one of the neighbours would knock at the door to find out whether I'd died and yes, I wanted to say, I'm slowly rotting, smelling bad or not smelling at all like ordinary people do when they die, waiting for a happiness that never comes. They wouldn't understand, no one would understand. I didn't understand in those days, do you?

Dragons, as I said, can't stand ugliness. He'd leave when that smell of rotten fruit, flowers and, worst of all, feelings became unbearable, matching the smell of the happiness he had once again failed to bring me. Asleep or awake, I took his departure like a sudden punch in the chest. Then I'd look up and around, in search of God or something like that: wood nymphs, archangels, radioactive clouds, demons or whatever. I never saw them. I never saw anything apart from the walls that were suddenly so empty without him.

Only someone who's had a dragon in their home can know how deserted this house seems after he's gone. Dunes, glaciers, steppes. No more greenish reflections in the corners ever again, no aroma of herbs in the air, no more coloured smoke or shapes like serpents peeping through the cracks in half-opened doors. Sadder still; no more desire inside you to be happy ever again, even if that happiness leaves you with your heart beating wildly, your hands clammy, your eyes shining and that hunger when you can't swallow anything. Except for that loveliness which is seeing, not chewing, and for that very reason is a form of discomfort too. In the barren dimness of a house emptied of the presence of a dragon, even as you start to eat and sleep normally again, as ordinary people do, you no longer know whether that old swamp that was full of unrealised possibilities might not be preferable to this barrenness now. When everything, without him, is nothing.

Today I think I know. Does a dragon come and go away again so that your world will grow? I ask this because I'm not sure, perhaps things are rather elementary, for example, does a dragon come and go away again so that you will learn about the pain of not having him, after cherishing the illusion of possessing him? So that human beings will learn how to hold on to him, if he comes back one day?

No, that's not how it is. That's not right.

Dragons don't stay. Dragons are just the announcement of themselves. They are forever rehearsing, and never make their debut. The curtains never actually open so that they can go on stage. They give a glimpse of themselves and then go up in smoke without ever revealing their shape. Applause would be unbearable for them; the confirmation that their nonconformity is understood and accepted and admired, and therefore – the wrong way round, the same as the right way round – misunderstood, rejected, despised. Dragons don't want to be accepted. They flee from paradise, the paradise that we ordinary people invent; the way I invented a wondrous world of tricks to await him and trap him here with me forever. Dragons have no knowledge of a paradise where everything goes perfectly and nothing hurts or sparkles or gasps in an eternal monotony of peaceable falseness. Their paradise is conflict, never harmony.

When I think about him again, on those nights when I've taken to leaning out of the window looking for moving lights in the sky, I like to imagine him flying along with his big golden wings, free in space, heading for everywhere which is nowhere. That is his more subtle nature, averse to the paradisiacal prisons that I was stupidly preparing for him with snares of flowers, fruits and ribbons when he came. Artificial paradises that gradually rotted, my own paradise – so ordinary and thirsty – tolerating all of his extravagances, which must sound ridiculous, pathetic and wretched to you. Now I just glide about, not too desperate about being happy.

The mornings are nice to wake up in, drink coffee, watch the time go by. Objects are nice to look at, they don't give you too many frights because they are what they are and they look at us too, with eyes that are thinking nothing. Since I sent him away, so that I could at last learn about the great disillusionment of paradise, that's how I've been feeling – hardly feeling at all.

All that's left is this story I'm telling, are you still listening? The odd note on the table, full ashtrays, empty glasses and this paper napkin where I noted down some apparently wise phrases about love and God, together with a sentence I'm afraid to decipher and which maybe, after all, just says something simple such as, none of this exists. And that nothing would include love and God, and dragons too and all the rest, visible or invisible.

None of this, none of it exists.

Then I'm almost sick and weep and bleed when I think these things. But I breathe deeply, rub my hands together and generate an energy from within. To keep myself alive, I go out in search of illusions like the smell of herbs or greenish reflections of scales around the flat and when I find them, even if it's just in my mind's eye, then again I become able to claim, as if it were a harmless vice – I've got a dragon living with me. And in this way I begin a new story which this time *will* be absolutely true even if it's a total lie. I get tired of the love I feel and with a huge effort which gradually turns into a kind of modest joy, late in the evening, alone in the flat in the middle of a town where dragons are scarce, over and over I repeat this confused apprenticeship of mine for the child-who-is-me sitting anguished and cold on the knees of the calm old-man-who-is-me:

'Go to sleep, only dreams exist. Go to sleep, my child. Let it be sweet.'

No, that's not true either.

The Toy Catalogue by Sandra Petrignani

Sandra Petrignani explores the sensual and melancholy side of childhood in her witty and *simpatico* book, 'the Toy Catalogue'. She describes sixty-odd different toys and games, a little in the tradition of Georges Perec or Roland Barthes but with a special Italian warmth and ingenuity. This young writer has had great critical success in Italy and is now available in English for the first time in the 'Boulevard Italians' series.

'The toy catalogue: enjoyable, lighthearted, sometimes sad…' Il Messaggero
'by an extraordinary achievement of memory she restores to us the magical territory of play.'
L'Europeo

Boulevard Italian series. 128 pages £5.95
ISBN 0 946889 23 6

Boulevard books are published in the UK with Olive Press/Impact Books and distributed by Harrap Publishing Group.